Grafted into His Heart

Comfort for the Wild Branch

Dana Howard

Grafted Into His Heart: Comfort for the Wild Branch

Scripture quotations are drawn from various translations of the Holy Bible, as noted throughout the book. Some verses are paraphrased or adapted for clarity and devotional emphasis. All emphasis in Scripture quotations is the author's.

Printed in the United States of America

First Edition

For every wild branch that ever wondered if they belonged—

you do.

You always did.

He grafted you in with His own hands.

PREFACE

There are seasons when the heart feels like a wild branch — reaching, longing, trying to find where it belongs. I've lived through those seasons. Maybe you have too.

This book was born out of a time when I felt disconnected in ways I couldn't explain. I wasn't running from God, but I wasn't sure how to draw close either. My heart felt untethered, unsure, and tired from trying to hold itself together.

And in that quiet, aching place, God began to reveal Himself to me as the Gardener — not distant or demanding, but tender, patient, and deeply attentive. He showed me that I wasn't meant to grow alone. I wasn't meant to survive on my own strength. I wasn't meant to figure out how to heal myself.

He was drawing me into His heart with the same care a gardener uses when grafting a fragile branch into a living vine. Not forcefully. Not hurriedly. But with a love that knows exactly how to make the broken places whole again.

That's what it means to be grafted into His heart. It's when God takes the parts of us that feel disconnected or unworthy and joins them to Himself so closely that His life becomes our life. His strength becomes our strength. His love becomes the place we finally rest.

These pages are the story of that journey — not a lesson to master, but a relationship to receive. Each chapter is written as a tender word from the Gardener because that is how He met me: personally, gently, and with a voice that spoke straight into the places I didn't know how to open.

If you've ever felt like you don't belong… If you've ever wondered where your heart fits… If you've ever carried wounds that made you question your worth… Then this book is for you.

My prayer is that as you read, you'll feel the nearness of the One who has been tending your heart all along. The One who knows how to graft what feels wild and weary into a love that will never let you go.

May these words meet you gently. May they remind you that you are wanted. And may you discover, as I did, that the Gardener has been holding you close to His heart far longer than you ever realized.

With love,

Dana

From the Heart of the Gardener

I see you, beloved one. You've been trying to hold yourself together for so long, stretching toward hope while carrying more weight than your heart was meant to bear. You've wondered if anyone notices the cracks, the weariness, the quiet ache you tuck beneath your smile.

I notice. I always have.

You are not a burden to Me. You are not too much, too broken, or too far gone. You are a branch I have watched with tenderness, even in the seasons when you felt wild and alone.

Come rest here for a while. Let Me tend the places that hurt. Let Me steady what feels unsteady. Let Me draw you close enough to feel My heartbeat again.

You were never meant to grow alone. You were made to be grafted into My heart—held, nourished, and made whole in the safety of My hands.

I am with you now. And I will walk with you through every page that follows.

…for God is able to graft them in again.

Romans 11:23

PART ONE

The Wild Branch

God saw you before you knew Him. Even when you were wild, untamed, growing in rocky soil—He had His eye on you. You were never invisible. You were never too far.

CHAPTER 1

I Saw You First

From the Gardener

Beloved, before you ever turned your face toward Me, I was already looking at you. Before you whispered your first prayer, before you opened your first Bible, before you even knew My name—I saw you. I saw you growing wild on that rocky hillside, and My heart was already set on you.

You think you found Me, but the truth is I found you long before that. I watched you push your roots into difficult ground, fighting for every inch of life, and I thought, *There. That one. That is the branch I will graft into My heart.* You were never a stranger to Me. Even when the whole world walked past you without a second glance, I stopped. I knelt down. I called you by name.

Do not believe the lie that you came to Me too late, or that you were ever outside the reach of My love. I saw you first, dear one. Before the foundation of the world, I chose you. And nothing—nothing in all creation—could have kept Me from coming for you.

You were always the one I wanted. Even then. Even now. Especially now.

Before I formed you in the womb I knew you, before you were born I set you apart.

Jeremiah 1:5

Dear Lord, thank You for seeing me before I ever saw You. Thank You for choosing me when I did not even know I needed choosing. Help me believe today that I was never invisible to You—that Your eyes have been on me from the very beginning. I love You. Amen.

CHAPTER 2

Even Then

From the Gardener

My child, I know there are moments in your past that you cannot bring yourself to look at. Dark corners of your story where you are certain I could not have been present. You think, *Surely He was not there. Surely He turned away.*

But I was there, beloved. Even then. In the darkest room of your darkest night, I was there. When you could not feel Me, when you could not find Me, when you were convinced that you were utterly alone—My hand was on your back, steadying you. My breath was in your lungs, keeping you alive. I never left. I never even looked away.

There is no valley so deep that My presence does not reach the bottom of it. There is no night so black that My love cannot find you in it. You may not have known I was there, but I was. I always was. And I always will be.

Even then, beloved. Especially then.

Where can I go from your Spirit? Where can I flee from your presence? If I go up to the heavens, you are there; if I make my bed in the depths, you are there. If I rise on the wings of the dawn, if I settle on the far side of the sea, even there your hand will guide me, your right hand will hold me fast.

Psalm 139:7–10

Jesus, I confess that I have believed the lie that You abandoned me in my darkest moments. Forgive me for doubting Your presence. Open my eyes to see that You were there all along—holding me, breathing life into me, refusing to let me go. Thank You for never leaving. Amen.

CHAPTER 3

Wild but Not Forgotten

From the Gardener

You grew up wild, precious one. I know that. You grew in places that were not gentle, in soil that was not rich, under skies that were not always kind. And somewhere along the way, you began to believe that wild meant forgotten. That because no one tended you, no one wanted you.

But being wild never made you invisible to Me. I do not only love the branches that grew in manicured gardens. I love the ones that pushed through stone. I love the ones that bent in the wind and refused to break. I love *you*—exactly as you are, exactly where you have been.

While you were still far from Me, while you were still tangled in thorns and reaching in the wrong direction, I loved you. Not a distant, theoretical love. A love that got on its knees in the dirt beside you. A love that bled for you before you ever asked it to.

Wild does not mean unwanted, dear one. It just means I had to come a little farther to reach you. And I would do it again a thousand times.

But God demonstrates his own love for us in this: While we were still sinners, Christ died for us.

Romans 5:8

Father, I have spent so much of my life believing that I was forgotten because I was wild. Today I receive the truth that You loved me even when I was far away. Thank You for coming to find me. Thank You for loving me before I was lovable. Amen.

CHAPTER 4

The Soil You Came From

From the Gardener

I know you carry shame about where you started, beloved. The family you came from. The neighborhood. The choices that were made for you before you were old enough to make your own. You look at your roots and you think, *Nothing good could come from this soil.*

But I am not a God who judges the branch by the ground it grew in. I judge the branch by the fruit it will bear once it is grafted into Me. Your beginning does not determine your ending. Your soil does not define your harvest. I am the one who takes the wild thing from the hard ground and plants it in a garden of grace.

Look at Abraham. I pulled him from a land of idols. Look at Ruth. She came from a people who did not know My name. And yet I wove them both into the very lineage of My Son. I specialize in making something beautiful from unlikely beginnings.

Do not be ashamed of where you started, dear one. Be amazed at where I am taking you.

Look to the rock from which you were cut and to the quarry from which you were hewn; look to Abraham, your father, and to Sarah, who gave you birth.

Isaiah 51:1–2

Lord, I give You the shame I carry about my past. I release the lie that my beginnings disqualify me from Your purpose. You are the God of unlikely stories, and I trust that mine is no exception. Write something beautiful with my life. Amen.

CHAPTER 5

I Knew Your Name

From the Gardener

Before your mother chose your name, I already knew it. Before your birth certificate was signed, before anyone on earth spoke it aloud, I whispered it in the halls of heaven. Your name was on My lips before it was ever on theirs.

You are not a number to Me, beloved. You are not a case file or a statistic or a face in the crowd. You are a name—a name that I chose, a name that I love, a name that I call out in the quiet of the morning and the stillness of the night.

When the world makes you feel anonymous, when loneliness wraps itself around you and tells you that no one truly knows you—remember this: I know your name. I know the sound of your heartbeat. I know the exact number of hairs on your head. I know you more intimately than you know yourself.

And I have called you Mine.

Fear not, for I have redeemed you; I have called you by name, you are mine.

Isaiah 43:1

Jesus, thank You for knowing my name. Thank You that I am not lost in the crowd to You. When I feel invisible and unknown, remind me that You see me, You know me, and You call me Yours. That is enough. Amen.

CHAPTER 6

You Were Never an Accident

From the Gardener

I need you to hear this, dear one, because I know the thought has crossed your mind more than once: *Maybe I was a mistake. Maybe I was not supposed to be here.* The enemy has whispered it. Perhaps even people you trusted have said it. But it is a lie, and I want to silence it right now.

You were not an accident. You were not a cosmic coincidence. You were fearfully and wonderfully made—every cell, every fingerprint, every beat of your heart was designed with intention. I formed you in secret and I called it good.

The world may not have been ready for you. The circumstances around your arrival may have been imperfect. But My plan for you has never been anything less than purposeful. You were made on purpose, for a purpose, by a God who does not make mistakes.

You belong here, beloved. You were always meant to be here.

For you created my inmost being; you knit me together in my mother's womb. I praise you because I am fearfully and wonderfully made; your works are wonderful, I know that full well.

Psalm 139:13–14

Father, I reject the lie that I was an accident. You made me with Your own hands and You called me wonderful. Help me to walk in that truth today—to see myself the way You see me: fearfully and wonderfully made. Amen.

CHAPTER 7

The Wind That Carried You

From the Gardener

You have known some fierce winds, haven't you, beloved? Storms that bent you nearly to the ground. Gusts that ripped away things you thought you could not live without. You have been battered and shaken and blown in directions you never intended to go.

But what if I told you that even the wind was under My command? What if the very storms that blew you off course were the ones I used to carry you to Me? Not every wind is punishment, dear one. Sometimes the wind that uproots you is the same wind that plants you somewhere better.

I am the Lord of the storm. I speak to the wind and it obeys. And even when it howled around you, even when you could not hear My voice above the roar—I was the one directing it. I was the one making sure it carried you, not destroyed you.

The winds have died down now. Rest, beloved. You are safe.

Then they cried out to the Lord in their trouble, and he brought them out of their distress. He stilled the storm to a whisper; the waves of the sea were hushed.

Psalm 107:28–30

Lord, I give You every storm that has ever shaken me. I trust that You were in the wind, guiding me even when I could not see Your hand. Thank You for carrying me through. Help me rest now in Your stillness. Amen.

CHAPTER 8

I Counted Every Tear

From the Gardener

My precious child, do you know what I did with every tear you cried? I kept them. Every single one. The ones that fell on your pillow at three in the morning. The ones you blinked back in the grocery store because you did not want anyone to see. The ones you cried in the shower so no one could hear. I collected them all.

Your grief was never invisible to Me. Your pain was never wasted in My sight. I kept a record of every sleepless night, every whispered prayer, every moment your heart broke into a piece so small you thought it could never be put back together.

I did not keep your tears to remind you of your suffering. I kept them because they are precious to Me. They are evidence that your heart is alive, that it still feels, that it still hopes. A heart that can weep is a heart that can heal.

Cry if you need to, beloved. I am catching every drop.

You keep track of all my sorrows. You have collected all my tears in your bottle. You have recorded each one in your book.

Psalm 56:8

Jesus, thank You for seeing every tear I have ever cried. Thank You that none of my pain has been invisible to You. I give You the grief I have been carrying alone. Hold it for me. Hold me. Amen.

CHAPTER 9

Tangled but Treasured

From the Gardener

I see the tangles, dear one. The confusion. The knots of regret and fear and what-ifs that have wound themselves around your heart. I see how you look at yourself and think, *What a mess. Who could love this mess?*

I could. I do. Your tangles do not diminish your treasure. You are like a pearl still caked in sand—the grit does not change the value of what is underneath. I look at you and I do not see the mess. I see the masterpiece beneath it, waiting to be revealed.

You do not have to untangle yourself before you come to Me. Come tangled. Come confused. Come with your knots and your questions and your doubts all wound together. I am patient enough to work through every one of them with you. And while I do, I will hold you close, because you are precious in My eyes, tangled or not.

You are treasured, beloved. Exactly as you are.

Since you are precious and honored in my sight, and because I love you, I will give people in exchange for you, nations in exchange for your life.

Isaiah 43:4

Father, I come to You tangled and messy. I do not have it all together, and I am learning that I do not need to. Thank You for treasuring me even in the middle of my mess. Untangle me gently, Lord. I trust Your hands. Amen.

CHAPTER 10

Before the World Began

From the Gardener

Beloved, I want to take you back to the beginning—not the beginning of your life, but the beginning of everything. Before the first star was flung into the sky. Before the oceans found their edges. Before time itself drew its first breath. I was there, and so were you—in My mind, in My heart, in My plan.

You were chosen before the foundation of the world. Not as an afterthought. Not as a backup plan. You were first-draft, original-design, on-purpose chosen. I looked out over the vast expanse of all that would ever be, and I chose you to be Mine.

The enemy will try to make you feel like a late addition, like you barely made the cut. But the truth is, your name was written before the ink of creation was dry. You are ancient in My love. You are eternal in My purpose.

You have always been Mine, dear one. Always.

For he chose us in him before the creation of the world to be holy and blameless in his sight.

Ephesians 1:4

Lord, the idea that You chose me before the world began is almost too beautiful to believe. But I choose to believe it today. I am not an afterthought. I am not a mistake. I was chosen, and I am Yours. Thank You, Father. Amen.

CHAPTER 11

I Waited for You

From the Gardener

My child, you thought you were the one searching. You thought you were the one wandering, trying to find your way home. But the truth is, I was the one waiting. Standing at the edge of the garden. Watching the road. Hoping today would be the day you turned around.

I am the most patient Gardener. I do not rush the wild branch. I do not force it from the hillside. I wait. I watch. I tend the place in My garden where I know you will one day be planted, keeping the soil ready, keeping the space open. No one else could fill it. It was always yours.

And when you finally came—stumbling, uncertain, wondering if you were welcome—I did not stand at a distance with crossed arms. I ran to you. I ran, beloved. Because I had been waiting so long, and the sight of you walking toward Me was the most beautiful thing I had ever seen.

I would have waited forever. But I am so glad you came.

The Lord is not slow in keeping his promise, as some understand slowness. Instead he is patient with you, not wanting anyone to perish, but everyone to come to repentance.

2 Peter 3:9

Jesus, thank You for waiting for me. Thank You for never giving up, even when I took so long to come home. Your patience is more than I deserve and more than I can understand. I am here now. I am Yours. Amen.

CHAPTER 12

The Gardener's Eye

From the Gardener

Dear one, a good gardener does not choose branches at random. He walks the hillside with a practiced eye. He examines the grain of the wood, the angle of the growth, the strength hidden beneath rough bark. He knows which branch will take to the graft and which will not. He chooses with wisdom, with care, with love.

My Father is that Gardener. And He chose you. Not because you were the prettiest branch on the hill. Not because you were the strongest or the straightest. He chose you because He saw something in you that you could not yet see in yourself—a capacity for life, for growth, for bearing fruit that would nourish the world.

He was already planning where to place you. Already measuring the angle of the cut. Already preparing the place in the living tree where you would be bound and held until the graft took hold. Nothing was left to chance. Every detail was designed by Love.

You are the branch the Gardener chose, beloved. And His eye is still on you.

I am the true vine, and my Father is the gardener.

John 15:1

Father, thank You for being a Gardener who chooses with love. Thank You for seeing in me what I cannot yet see. I trust Your eye. I trust Your hands. I trust the place You have prepared for me. Amen.

PART TWO

The Cut

When everything falls apart. The pain of being separated from the old life. God's severity and kindness working together. Sometimes things have to be severed before they can be saved.

CHAPTER 13

The Kindness in the Cutting

From the Gardener

I know the cut was painful, beloved. I know it felt like everything was being ripped away. The life you knew, the ground you were rooted in, the identity you had built around yourself—all of it, severed in what felt like a single, cruel stroke.

But I need you to see what you could not see in that moment: there was kindness in the cutting. The old roots were not feeding you anymore. The soil you clung to was poisoned with things that would have slowly killed you—bitterness, fear, false comfort, self-destruction. I could not leave you there. Love would not allow it.

No discipline seems pleasant at the time. I know that. It seems painful. But afterward—oh, beloved, the afterward—it produces a harvest of righteousness and peace. The cut was not cruelty. The cut was rescue.

One day you will look back at the place where the blade fell and you will see not a wound but a doorway. A doorway into everything I had planned for you.

No discipline seems pleasant at the time, but painful. Later on, however, it produces a harvest of righteousness and peace for those who have been trained by it.

Hebrews 12:11

Lord, the cut hurt. I will not pretend it didn't. But I am beginning to see Your kindness in it. Help me trust that what felt like cruelty was actually rescue. Help me walk through the doorway You have opened. Amen.

CHAPTER 14

Let Go of the Old Roots

From the Gardener

Dear one, I see you reaching back. I see you longing for the familiar ground, even though it was the ground that was starving you. The old roots feel safe because they are known. But known does not always mean good. Familiar does not always mean life-giving.

I am asking you to let go. Not because the past did not matter, but because the future I have for you requires both of your hands. You cannot hold onto the old and receive the new at the same time. You cannot be grafted into the living tree while you are still clinging to dead soil.

I know it is frightening. I know it feels like free-falling. But I am beneath you, beloved. I am the net, the ground, the arms that will catch you. Let go of what was. I am doing something new—can you not see it? It is already springing up. But you have to release the old to take hold of it.

Open your hands, precious one. What I am placing in them is better than anything you are letting go of.

Forget the former things; do not dwell on the past. See, I am doing a new thing! Now it springs up; do you not perceive it?

Isaiah 43:18–19

Father, give me the courage to let go. I have been holding onto things that are no longer feeding me, afraid that there will be nothing to replace them. I open my hands today. Fill them with something new. Fill them with You. Amen.

CHAPTER 15

It Had to Break

From the Gardener

I know you wish I could have gotten you here without the breaking. I know you wonder if there was another way—a gentler path, a less painful route. And I understand that question, beloved. I asked it Myself, in a garden, on My knees, with tears running down My face.

But some things have to break before they can be remade. The seed has to split open before the plant can grow. The shell has to crack before the chick can breathe. And sometimes the heart has to shatter before it can be reshaped into something large enough to hold the love I want to pour into it.

Your brokenness is not your disqualification. It is your qualification. I do not dwell in palaces. I dwell with the broken and the humble. I make My home in the shattered places, because that is where the light gets in.

You are not ruined, dear one. You are being remade.

My sacrifice, O God, is a broken spirit; a broken and contrite heart you, God, will not despise.

Psalm 51:17

Jesus, I bring You my broken pieces. I do not understand why it had to hurt so much, but I trust that You are using every fracture to make me new. Dwell in my brokenness, Lord. Let the light in. Amen.

CHAPTER 16

I Did Not Leave You in the Dirt

From the Gardener

Beloved, when the cut came and you fell, you thought that was the end. You lay there in the dirt, severed from everything you knew, and you waited for Me to walk away. Because that is what everyone else had done, wasn't it? They cut and they left. They broke and they moved on.

But I am not like them. I did not cut you and leave you lying on the ground. I cut you and I picked you up. I held you in My hands—carefully, tenderly, the way a surgeon holds something precious. Because you are not debris to Me. You are a living branch, and I had plans for you.

I will never leave you. I will never forsake you. Not in the dirt, not in the dark, not in the doubt. My hands are scarred, beloved—scarred from the nails I chose to bear so that I could hold you forever. And these scarred hands will never, ever let you go.

Be strong and courageous. Do not be afraid or terrified because of them, for the Lord your God goes with you; he will never leave you nor forsake you.

Deuteronomy 31:6

Lord, thank You for not leaving me in the dirt. Thank You for picking me up when I was sure I had been abandoned. I trust Your scarred hands. I trust that You will never let me go. Amen.

CHAPTER 17

The Night Before the Garden

From the Gardener

This is the darkest hour, isn't it, dear one? The night that seems like it will never end. You are between what was and what will be, suspended in a place where you can see neither the past nor the future. And the darkness is so thick you can almost feel it pressing against your skin.

I know this night. I spent one like it in a garden called Gethsemane. I know what it is to weep so hard your tears mix with blood. I know what it is to cry out for relief and hear only silence. I know. And because I know, I can sit with you in it without flinching.

But hear Me, beloved: the morning is coming. Weeping may stay for the night, but joy comes in the morning. This darkness is not permanent. It is the final hour before the dawn, and when the sun rises, you will see what I have been preparing while you slept in the dark.

Hold on, precious one. Just a little longer. The garden is almost ready.

For his anger lasts only a moment, but his favor lasts a lifetime; weeping may stay for the night, but rejoicing comes in the morning.

Psalm 30:5

Jesus, I am in the dark night. I cannot see the morning. But I believe You when You say it is coming. Give me strength to hold on just a little longer. Stay with me in this darkness. You are my only light. Amen.

CHAPTER 18

Severed but Safe

From the Gardener

You feel severed from everything, don't you, beloved? Cut off from the familiar. Disconnected from the people and places and patterns that once defined you. You feel like a branch lying on the ground, separated from the only tree you ever knew.

But severed does not mean unsafe. You are in My hands now, and My hands are the safest place in the universe. Nothing can touch you here that has not first passed through My fingers. Nothing can harm you here that I have not already overcome.

I know it does not feel safe. I know your heart is racing and your mind is spinning and everything in you is screaming to go back to what you knew. But what you knew was killing you, dear one. And what I have for you is life—abundant, overflowing, more-than-you-can-imagine life.

You are severed from the old. But you are safe in the new. You are safe in Me.

So do not fear, for I am with you; do not be dismayed, for I am your God. I will strengthen you and help you; I will uphold you with my righteous right hand.

Isaiah 41:10

Father, I feel severed and scared. But I choose to believe that I am safe in Your hands. Quiet my racing heart. Steady my spinning mind. Remind me that Your righteous right hand is holding me right now. Amen.

CHAPTER 19

What You Lost Was Not Wasted

From the Gardener

I see the inventory of losses you carry, dear one. The years you feel were stolen. The relationships that crumbled. The dreams that turned to dust. You look at the wreckage and you think, *It was all for nothing.*

But I am a God who wastes nothing. Not a single tear. Not a single sleepless night. Not a single wrong turn. In My hands, even the losses become raw materials for something beautiful. The compost of your pain becomes the soil for your future harvest.

I work all things together for good—not some things, not the pretty things, not the things that make sense. *All* things. Even the ugly ones. Even the ones that feel irredeemable. I am the God who turns ashes into gardens and graves into doorways.

Nothing you have been through is wasted, beloved. I am using every bit of it.

And we know that in all things God works for the good of those who love him, who have been called according to his purpose.

Romans 8:28

Lord, I give You my losses. I give You the years, the relationships, the dreams that fell apart. I trust You to waste nothing. Make something beautiful from the wreckage of my story. I believe You can. Amen.

CHAPTER 20

I Carried You Through the Fire

From the Gardener

Beloved, you walked through fire. I know you did. I was there. I felt the heat on My own skin because I was walking beside you, step for step, breath for breath. You thought you were alone in the flames, but you were never alone. Not for one second.

The fire was real. The pain was real. I will not minimize what you endured. But I need you to notice something: you came through. The flames did not consume you. The smoke did not suffocate you. You are standing here, reading these words, breathing, alive—and that is not because you are strong. It is because I carried you.

When you pass through the waters, I am with you. When you walk through the fire, you will not be burned. This is not a metaphor, dear one. This is My promise. And I have never broken a promise.

When you pass through the waters, I will be with you; and when you pass through the rivers, they will not sweep over you. When you walk through the fire, you will not be burned; the flames will not set you ablaze.

Isaiah 43:2

Jesus, You carried me through the fire. I did not make it on my own strength—I made it because You were with me. Thank You for walking into the flames for me. Thank You that I am still here. Amen.

CHAPTER 21

The Wound That Heals

From the Gardener

Every graft requires a wound, beloved. The branch must be cut and the tree must be opened. Two wounds meeting—that is how the graft takes hold. The living wood of the tree touches the living wood of the branch, and where there was once pain, new life begins to flow.

My wounds healed you. The stripes on My back, the nails in My hands, the spear in My side—those wounds became the opening in the tree through which you were grafted in. My pain made room for your life. My blood became the sap that nourishes you still.

And your wound? The place where you were cut? That wound is healing, too. Not disappearing—healing. It will become the very place where you are most alive, most connected, most fruitful. The scar will remain, but it will tell a story of rescue, not ruin.

The wound is not the end of your story, dear one. It is the beginning of your grafting.

He himself bore our sins in his body on the cross, so that we might die to sins and live for righteousness; by his wounds you have been healed.

1 Peter 2:24

Lord, I see it now—Your wounds and mine, meeting in the graft. Thank You for bearing the pain that made my healing possible. I trust that my wound is not the end. It is the beginning. Heal me, Lord. Amen.

CHAPTER 22

Trust the Gardener's Hands

From the Gardener

I know you do not understand what I am doing, beloved. I know this process feels confusing and painful and nothing like what you imagined. You want to see the blueprint. You want to know the plan. You want a timeline and a guarantee and a map with every turn clearly marked.

But I am asking you for something harder than understanding. I am asking you for trust. Trust the hands that hold you, even when you cannot see where they are taking you. Trust the Gardener, even when the garden makes no sense yet.

My ways are higher than yours. My thoughts are higher than yours. Not because I am distant, but because I can see what you cannot. I can see the tree you will become. I can see the fruit you will bear. I can see the lives that will be nourished by the branch that is, right now, crying out in pain.

Trust Me, dear one. I have never lost a graft.

Trust in the Lord with all your heart and lean not on your own understanding; in all your ways submit to him, and he will make your paths straight.

Proverbs 3:5–6

Father, I do not understand. But I choose to trust. I choose to believe that Your hands are good, even when Your plan is hidden. I surrender my need to understand and I lean into Your wisdom. Lead me, Lord. Amen.

CHAPTER 23

Stripped Down to the Heartwood

From the Gardener

My child, I know it feels like everything has been stripped away. The titles, the roles, the masks, the performances—all gone. You stand before Me bare, with nothing left to hide behind, and you feel more vulnerable than you have ever felt in your life.

But this is not punishment. This is preparation. A grafted branch must be stripped down to the heartwood—the innermost, truest part of itself—so that it can bond with the living tree. The bark, the outer layers, the parts that were hardened by weather and time—they have to go. Only the heartwood can receive the sap.

What remains when everything else is stripped away? The essential you. The you I created. The you that exists beneath every mask you ever wore. And that you—that raw, real, unadorned you—is the one I love most. That is the one I have been trying to reach all along.

You are not diminished, beloved. You are finally uncovered.

Therefore we do not lose heart. Though outwardly we are wasting away, yet inwardly we are being renewed day by day. For our light and momentary troubles are achieving for us an eternal glory that far outweighs them all.

2 Corinthians 4:16–18

Jesus, I feel stripped bare. But I choose to see it as uncovering rather than destruction. You are reaching my heartwood—the truest part of me. I offer it to You. Bond me to the living tree. Amen.

CHAPTER 24

You Are Not Ruined

From the Gardener

I can hear the thought that loops through your mind like a broken record: *I am ruined. It is too late. Too much has happened. Too much has been lost.* And I understand why you think that, beloved. When you look at the landscape of your life through human eyes, it does look like devastation.

But I do not see with human eyes. Where you see ruin, I see renovation. Where you see an ending, I see a beginning. Where you see ashes, I see the foundation for something so beautiful it would take your breath away if you could see it now.

I am the God who makes all things new. Not some things. All things. Including you. Including your story. Including the chapters you wish you could tear out and burn. I do not work around your brokenness. I work through it. I work *with* it. I make it the cornerstone of something extraordinary.

You are not ruined, dear one. You are under construction. And the Builder knows exactly what He is doing.

'For I know the plans I have for you,' declares the Lord, 'plans to prosper you and not to harm you, plans to give you hope and a future.'

Jeremiah 29:11

Lord, I have been telling myself I am ruined. Today I choose to hear Your voice instead. I am not ruined—I am under renovation. You have plans for me, and they are good. I trust the Builder. Amen.

PART THREE

Grafted In

The miraculous moment of being grafted into the cultivated tree. Chosen contrary to nature. Placed deliberately by God's own hands into something living, something nourishing.

CHAPTER 25

Contrary to Nature

From the Gardener

Here is the miracle, beloved: what I did with you should not have worked. By every law of nature, a wild olive branch grafted into a cultivated tree should fail. The wood is different. The grain is different. The sap should reject it. Nature says it cannot be done.

But I am not bound by nature. I am the one who made nature, and I can overrule it whenever I choose. I specialize in doing what cannot be done. I part seas. I raise the dead. I graft wild branches into the living tree and I make them thrive.

You were not supposed to belong here—not by the world's standards. You were too rough, too wild, too different. But I took you and I placed you where you had no right to be, and I said, *This one is Mine now. The sap of My life will flow through this branch.* And it did. And it does. And it always will.

You are a miracle, dear one. Contrary to nature. Sustained by grace.

After all, if you were cut out of an olive tree that is wild by nature, and contrary to nature were grafted into a cultivated olive tree, how much more readily will these, the natural branches, be grafted into their own olive tree!

Romans 11:24

Lord, I am a miracle. I should not be here, but You put me here. Against all odds, against all nature, You grafted me in. I will never stop being amazed by that. Thank You for doing the impossible with my life. Amen.

CHAPTER 26

I Chose You

From the Gardener

Let this sink deep, beloved: you did not choose Me. I chose you. Not the other way around. Before you made your decision, I had already made Mine. Before you said yes, I had already said *yours*.

You were not selected from a lineup. You were not picked last. You were chosen first—deliberately, joyfully, irrevocably. I looked at you and I wanted you. Not a cleaned-up version of you. Not a future version of you. You—as you were, where you were, with everything you carried.

The world makes you audition for belonging. You have to prove yourself, earn your place, perform well enough to stay. But My kingdom does not work that way. In My kingdom, belonging is a gift, not a reward. And I have already given it to you.

You are chosen, dear one. Let that word settle into the deepest part of your heart and stay there forever.

You did not choose me, but I chose you and appointed you so that you might go and bear fruit—fruit that will last.

John 15:16

Jesus, You chose me. Not because I earned it, not because I deserved it, but because You wanted me. I receive that truth today. I am chosen. I am wanted. I am Yours. Amen.

CHAPTER 27

Placed by My Own Hands

From the Gardener

I did not delegate this, beloved. I did not hand you off to an angel or leave your placement to chance. I placed you Myself. With My own hands—the hands that shaped the mountains and scooped out the seas—I took you, and I set you exactly where you are.

Your place in the tree was not random. I measured it. I prepared it. I knew exactly which spot would give you the most sunlight, the most shelter, the most nourishment from the root. I placed you with the precision of a surgeon and the tenderness of a father laying his newborn in a crib.

When you feel out of place, when you wonder if you ended up in the wrong spot, remember this: the Lord has assigned your portion and your cup. The boundary lines have fallen for you in pleasant places. You are exactly where I want you to be.

Lord, you alone are my portion and my cup; you make my lot secure. The boundary lines have fallen for me in pleasant places; surely I have a delightful inheritance.

Psalm 16:5–6

Father, thank You for placing me with Your own hands. When I doubt my position, remind me that You are the one who chose this spot for me. I trust Your placement. I trust Your precision. I trust Your love. Amen.

CHAPTER 28

You Belong Here

From the Gardener

I know the whisper you hear, beloved. The one that hisses in your ear every time you walk into a room full of believers, every time you open a hymnal, every time you bow your head to pray: *You do not belong here. You are an imposter. They will find you out.*

That voice is a liar. You are not an outsider in My family. You are not a guest who might be asked to leave. You are a citizen of My kingdom, a member of My household, built on the foundation of the apostles and prophets, with Christ Jesus Himself as the cornerstone.

You belong here. Not because you earned it, but because I declared it. Not because you are perfect, but because I am. And when I say you belong, no voice in hell or on earth has the authority to say otherwise.

Sit down, dear one. Take off your coat. You are home.

Consequently, you are no longer foreigners and strangers, but fellow citizens with God's people and also members of his household.

Ephesians 2:19

Lord, silence the voice that tells me I do not belong. I am not a foreigner. I am not a stranger. I am a citizen of Your kingdom and a member of Your household. I belong here. Help me live like I believe it. Amen.

CHAPTER 29

The Sap Begins to Flow

From the Gardener

Can you feel it, beloved? Something is happening beneath the surface. Something quiet and deep and alive. The sap of the living tree is beginning to flow into you—My life, My nourishment, My strength, seeping into the dry places of your soul like water into parched ground.

This is what it feels like to be connected to Me. It does not always come as a thunderbolt or a burning bush. Sometimes it comes as a gentle warmth, a quiet knowing, a peace that you cannot explain but cannot deny. The sap does not announce itself. It simply flows.

You have been running on your own strength for so long, dear one. You have been trying to produce life from your own resources, and you have been running dry. But you are connected to the root now. You do not have to manufacture life anymore. Just receive it. Let it flow.

The sap is flowing, beloved. Let it reach every dry branch, every withered leaf, every starving cell of your being.

So then, just as you received Christ Jesus as Lord, continue to live your lives in him, rooted and built up in him, strengthened in the faith as you were taught, and overflowing with thankfulness.

Colossians 2:6–7

Jesus, I feel it—Your life flowing into mine. I have been running on empty for so long. Today I stop striving and I start receiving. Fill every dry place in me with Your living sap. I am rooted in You. Amen.

CHAPTER 30

No Longer Wild

From the Gardener

You keep calling yourself wild, beloved. You keep looking in the mirror and seeing the branch from the rocky hillside. But I need you to see what I see: you are not wild anymore. You are grafted. You are connected. You are fed by the same root that feeds every other branch in My tree.

The old identity is gone. The one who was defined by chaos and survival and scarcity—that is not who you are anymore. You are a new creation. The old has passed away. The new has come. And the new is more beautiful than you can imagine.

Stop introducing yourself by your past. Stop wearing your old labels like name tags. You are not your addiction. You are not your abuse. You are not your worst mistake. You are in Christ, and in Christ, everything is made new.

You were wild once. But that is not your name anymore.

Therefore, if anyone is in Christ, the new creation has come: The old has gone, the new is here!

2 Corinthians 5:17

Father, I release my old identity today. I am not who I used to be. I am a new creation in Christ. Help me stop defining myself by my past and start living in the newness You have given me. I am Yours. Amen.

CHAPTER 31

Bound to the Living Tree

From the Gardener

When a gardener grafts a branch, he binds it tightly to the tree. He wraps it with care, sealing the wound, holding the branch in place until the graft takes hold. The branch cannot fall away because it is bound—held fast, held close, held secure.

That is what I have done with you, beloved. I have bound you to Myself with cords that cannot be broken. Not ropes of obligation or chains of guilt, but bands of love so strong that nothing in all creation can tear them apart. Neither death nor life, neither angels nor demons, neither the present nor the future, nor any powers, neither height nor depth, nor anything else in all creation can separate you from My love.

Nothing. Do you hear Me? Nothing.

You are bound to the living tree, and the living tree will never let you go.

For I am convinced that neither death nor life, neither angels nor demons, neither the present nor the future, nor any powers, neither height nor depth, nor anything else in all creation, will be able to separate us from the love of God that is in Christ Jesus our Lord.

Romans 8:38–39

Lord, nothing can separate me from Your love. Nothing. I let that truth wrap around me today like the bands that hold the graft in place. I am bound to You, and I am never letting go. Amen.

CHAPTER 32

The Graft Holds

From the Gardener

You keep testing the connection, don't you, beloved? Pulling at the graft to see if it will hold. Waiting for the day when My love gives out, when My grace runs dry, when I finally decide that this wild branch was not worth the trouble after all.

Stop pulling, dear one. The graft holds. What I have joined together cannot be undone. I give you eternal life, and you shall never perish. No one can snatch you from My hand. My Father, who has given you to Me, is greater than all, and no one can snatch you from My Father's hand.

Not your failures. Not your doubts. Not your worst day or your weakest moment. The graft holds. It held yesterday. It holds today. It will hold tomorrow and the day after that and the day after that and into eternity.

Stop testing it and start trusting it. The graft holds, beloved. I promise.

I give them eternal life, and they shall never perish; no one will snatch them out of my hand. My Father, who has given them to me, is greater than all; no one can snatch them out of my Father's hand.

John 10:28–29

Jesus, I confess that I have been testing the graft—pulling at Your love to see if it would hold. Forgive me. I choose to trust that what You have joined cannot be undone. The graft holds. I believe it. Amen.

CHAPTER 33

Welcome Home

From the Gardener

You have been away so long, beloved. Wandering in far countries, spending yourself on things that could not satisfy, eating husks meant for pigs while a feast was waiting for you at your Father's table. But you are here now. And I am so glad you are here.

I did not wait for you at the door with a lecture. I did not prepare a list of your failures to read aloud before I let you in. I saw you coming from a long way off, and I ran. I ran to you, beloved. I threw My arms around you and I kissed you and I called for the finest robe and the ring and the sandals and the fatted calf.

Because this is what homecoming looks like in My kingdom. Not shame. Not probation. Celebration. You were lost and now you are found. You were dead and now you are alive. And all of heaven is throwing a party because you are home.

Welcome home, dear one. Welcome home.

But while he was still a long way off, his father saw him and was filled with compassion for him; he ran to his son, threw his arms around him and kissed him.

Luke 15:20

Father, I am home. Thank You for running to me. Thank You for not meeting me with a lecture but with open arms. I do not deserve this welcome, but I receive it with a grateful heart. I am home. Amen.

CHAPTER 34

I Made Room for You

From the Gardener

Beloved, you did not have to squeeze yourself into My family. You did not have to shrink down to fit. I made room for you—spacious, generous, just-for-you room. I went ahead and prepared a place, and that place has your name on it. No one else can fill it.

In My Father's house there are many rooms. Many. Not cramped closets or temporary guest beds. Rooms. Permanent, beautiful, designed-with-you-in-mind rooms. You are not camping in the hallway, dear one. You have a place at the table. You have a chair with your name on the back of it.

The world has made you feel like there is never enough room. Not enough love to go around. Not enough grace to cover you. Not enough space for someone with your kind of story. But I am telling you: there is more than enough. I made room. I always make room.

My Father's house has many rooms; if that were not so, would I have told you that I am going there to prepare a place for you? And if I go and prepare a place for you, I will come back and take you to be with me that you also may be where I am.

John 14:2–3

Jesus, thank You for making room for me. Not squeezing me in as an afterthought, but preparing a place just for me. I receive the generous space of Your love today. There is enough. There is more than enough. Amen.

CHAPTER 35

You Fit Perfectly

From the Gardener

You have spent your whole life feeling like a misfit, haven't you, beloved? The odd one out. The square peg. The one who never quite belonged in any group, any family, any room. And you have started to believe that the problem is you—that you are simply too strange to fit anywhere.

But you fit perfectly in Me. God has placed the parts in the body, every one of them, just as He wanted them to be. You are not an extra piece left over after the puzzle was assembled. You are a critical, irreplaceable, perfectly shaped piece without which the picture would be incomplete.

Your quirks, your differences, the very things that made you feel like a misfit in the world—those are the things that make you fit perfectly in My kingdom. I designed you that way on purpose. You were never meant to fit in the world. You were meant to fit in Me.

But in fact God has placed the parts in the body, every one of them, just as he wanted them to be.

1 Corinthians 12:18

Father, I have felt like a misfit for so long. Today I choose to believe that I fit perfectly in Your plan. You designed me this way on purpose. I am not too much or too little—I am exactly right. Thank You. Amen

CHAPTER 36

The Miracle of Belonging

From the Gardener

Belonging is not something you earn, beloved. It is something you receive. It is a gift—pure, unmerited, wrapped in grace and tied with mercy. You cannot work hard enough to belong. You cannot be good enough to belong. You belong because I said so, and that is enough.

By grace you have been saved, through faith—and this is not from yourselves, it is the gift of God. Not by works, so that no one can boast. Your belonging is not a paycheck you earned. It is a love letter you opened. It is a miracle, and miracles cannot be manufactured.

So put down the scorecard. Stop tallying your good days against your bad days, trying to figure out if you have done enough to stay. You were grafted in by grace, and grace does not have an expiration date. You belong today, tomorrow, and forever—not because of anything you have done, but because of everything He has done.

Rest in the miracle, dear one. It is already yours.

For it is by grace you have been saved, through faith—and this is not from yourselves, it is the gift of God—not by works, so that no one can boast.

Ephesians 2:8–9

Lord, I put down the scorecard. I stop trying to earn what You have already given. I belong by grace, and grace is enough. Thank You for the miracle of belonging. I receive it with open hands. Amen.

PART FOUR

The Root Sustains You

Learning to draw nourishment from the root. Dependence on Christ. Being fed by something deeper than yourself—the sap, the life, the sustenance that flows from the ancient root.

CHAPTER 37

I Am Your Root

From the Gardener

Beloved, do not forget this: you do not support the root. The root supports you. You do not sustain Me. I sustain you. Every drop of life that flows through your veins, every breath of hope that fills your lungs, every moment of peace that settles over your heart—it all comes from Me.

I am the root that goes deeper than any drought can reach. I am the source that never runs dry. When the surface is parched and cracked and everything around you is withering, My roots are still drawing water from the deep places—places the drought cannot touch.

You do not have to be your own source, dear one. You were never designed to be. You were designed to draw from Me—daily, hourly, moment by moment. Let Me be your root. Let Me be the one who sustains you.

You are a branch. I am the root. And together, we are alive.

If some of the branches have been broken off, and you, though a wild olive shoot, have been grafted in among the others and now share in the nourishing sap from the olive root, do not consider yourself to be superior to those other branches. If you do, consider this: you do not support the root, but the root supports you.

Romans 11:17–18

Jesus, You are my root. I have been trying to sustain myself, and I am exhausted. Today I let You be my source. Feed me, sustain me, keep me alive. I draw from You and You alone. Amen.

CHAPTER 38

Draw from Me

From the Gardener

Come to Me, beloved. Come to Me when you are weary and burdened and carrying more than your shoulders were made to carry. Do not go to the world first. Do not go to the bottle or the screen or the busyness that numbs but never heals. Come to Me. I will give you rest.

I am not a last resort. I am the first refuge. I am not the emergency contact at the bottom of the list. I am the arms that should hold you first, before the weight gets too heavy, before the tears start falling, before the darkness closes in.

Draw from Me the way a branch draws sap from the root—naturally, continuously, without effort. It is not something you force. It is something you allow. Open yourself to My presence. Sit in My word. Breathe in My Spirit. And let the nourishment flow.

I have everything you need, dear one. Come and draw.

Come to me, all you who are weary and burdened, and I will give you rest.

Matthew 11:28

Lord, I come to You weary and burdened. I have been drawing from empty wells. Today I draw from You—the only source that never runs dry. Give me rest. Give me life. Give me You. Amen.

CHAPTER 39

Deep Calls to Deep

From the Gardener

There is a place inside you, beloved, that no surface thing can reach. A deep place. A hidden chamber of your heart where your truest longings live—the ache for meaning, the hunger for home, the thirst for something you cannot even name.

That deep place was made for Me. It is the place where My voice resonates, where My Spirit meets your spirit, where deep calls to deep in the roar of My waterfalls. The world tries to fill it with noise and distraction, but it was shaped for My presence alone. Nothing else fits.

I am calling to your depths right now, dear one. Can you hear it? Beneath the noise of your day, beneath the worries and the lists and the obligations—there is a sound like rushing water. That is Me. That is My Spirit, calling your spirit, inviting you deeper, always deeper.

Come deeper, beloved. The surface is not where life is found.

Deep calls to deep in the roar of your waterfalls; all your waves and breakers have swept over me.

Psalm 42:7

Father, I hear You calling from the deep places. I want to go deeper with You—past the surface, past the noise, into the place where Your Spirit meets mine. Take me deeper, Lord. I am listening. Amen.

CHAPTER 40

Rivers in the Desert

From the Gardener

My child, I know it feels like a desert right now. Dry. Barren. Endless. You look in every direction and see nothing but sand and heat and mirages that promise water but deliver dust. You are parched, and you have almost stopped hoping for rain.

But I am making a way in the desert. Right now, even as you read these words, I am carving rivers in the wasteland. I am splitting rocks and pouring out streams in places where water has never been. I am doing it for you, beloved, because you are Mine, and I will not let My branch wither.

The desert is not your destination. It is a passageway. And even in the passage, I provide. I do not wait until you reach the garden to start watering you. I water you in the desert. I sustain you in the wilderness. I am the God who gives rivers where there should be none.

Drink, beloved. The river is here.

See, I am doing a new thing! Now it springs up; do you not perceive it? I am making a way in the wilderness and streams in the wasteland. I provide water in the wilderness and streams in the wasteland, to give drink to my people, my chosen.

Isaiah 43:19–20

Lord, my soul is parched. But I believe You are making rivers in my desert. Open my eyes to see the water You are already providing. I drink from Your stream today. Sustain me, Lord. Amen.

CHAPTER 41

You Will Not Run Dry

From the Gardener

Dear one, you have been afraid of running out. Running out of strength. Running out of hope. Running out of faith. You have been rationing your joy like water in a canteen, taking tiny sips because you are terrified there will not be enough to get you through.

But you are connected to an unlimited supply now. The root that feeds you draws from the inexhaustible depths of God's love. It does not run dry in the summer. It does not freeze in the winter. It flows and flows and flows, and there is always more. Always.

Whoever drinks the water I give them will never thirst. It becomes a spring welling up to eternal life—not a puddle, not a trickle, but a spring. A source. An endless fountain bubbling up from the inside out.

You will not run dry, beloved. I am your spring. And I never, ever run out.

But whoever drinks the water I give them will never thirst. Indeed, the water I give them will become in them a spring of water welling up to eternal life.

John 4:14

Jesus, I have been rationing my hope, afraid there would not be enough. But You are a spring that never runs dry. I stop rationing and I start trusting. Fill me to overflowing, Lord. Amen.

CHAPTER 42

Be Still and Receive

From the Gardener

Beloved, stop striving. Stop running. Stop trying to earn what I am freely giving. Be still. Be still and know that I am God. Know it not just in your mind but in your bones, in your breath, in the quietest chamber of your heart.

A branch does not work to receive sap. It simply stays connected. It rests in its place on the tree, and the nourishment comes to it. That is what I am asking of you: not more effort, but more rest. Not more doing, but more being. Not more striving, but more stillness.

In the stillness, you will hear My voice. In the quiet, you will feel My presence. In the rest, you will receive strength you could never generate on your own. I am not impressed by your busyness, dear one. I am moved by your trust. And trust looks like stillness.

Be still. I am here. I am God. And I am taking care of everything.

Be still, and know that I am God; I will be exalted among the nations, I will be exalted in the earth.

Psalm 46:10

Father, I am so tired of striving. Today I choose stillness. I choose to rest in Your presence and receive what You are freely giving. I do not need to earn Your love. I need only to be still. Help me be still. Amen.

CHAPTER 43

My Strength in Your Weakness

From the Gardener

You think your weakness disqualifies you, beloved. You look at the places where you are frail, fragile, barely holding together, and you think, *I am not strong enough for this. I am not enough.*

But My grace is sufficient for you. My power is made perfect—not in your strength, but in your weakness. When you are at your weakest, that is when I am at My strongest. Because when you run out of your own power, you finally make room for Mine.

Your weakness is not something to be ashamed of. It is the window through which My strength enters your life. It is the opening in the branch through which the sap of the root flows in. If you were self-sufficient, you would not need Me. But you do need Me. And in that need, you find everything.

Boast in your weakness, dear one. For when you are weak, then you are truly strong.

But he said to me, 'My grace is sufficient for you, for my power is made perfect in weakness.' Therefore I will boast all the more gladly about my weaknesses, so that Christ's power may rest on me.

2 Corinthians 12:9

Lord, I stop hiding my weakness and I start offering it to You. Fill the weak places with Your power. Let Your strength flow through my fragile frame. I am weak, but in You, I am strong. Amen.

CHAPTER 44

Morning by Morning

From the Gardener

My mercies are new every morning, beloved. Every single morning. Not recycled, not leftover, not warmed-up versions of yesterday's grace. Brand new. Fresh. Made just for today's challenges, tailored to this morning's needs.

Yesterday's mercies were for yesterday. Tomorrow's mercies will be there tomorrow. But right now, this morning, I have poured out a fresh measure of grace that is perfectly calibrated for everything you will face today. It is enough. It is always enough.

Great is My faithfulness. Not great was or great will be. Great *is*—present tense, this moment, right now. I am faithful to you this morning and I will be faithful to you again when the sun rises tomorrow. You will never wake up to a day where My mercy has run out.

Good morning, dear one. My mercies are already waiting for you.

Because of the Lord's great love we are not consumed, for his compassions never fail. They are new every morning; great is your faithfulness.

Lamentations 3:22–23

Father, thank You for new mercies this morning. Thank You that Your compassions never fail, never run out, never expire. I receive today's grace with open hands and a grateful heart. Great is Your faithfulness. Amen.

CHAPTER 45

The Quiet Nourishment

From the Gardener

I do not always work in thunder and lightning, beloved. More often, I work in whispers. In the quiet turn of a season. In the slow growth of a root finding water underground. In the almost imperceptible moment when a bud forms on a branch that everyone thought was dead.

My most important work is often My quietest work. The sap that feeds you does not announce itself with trumpets. It moves silently, steadily, through channels hidden beneath the bark. You cannot see it, but it is there. You cannot hear it, but it is flowing. And it is keeping you alive.

Do not despise the quiet seasons, dear one. Do not mistake silence for absence. I am not gone just because you cannot hear Me shouting. I am here, in the still small voice, in the gentle whisper, doing the slow and sacred work of making you whole.

Listen closely, beloved. Not with your ears, but with your heart. I am speaking.

And after the earthquake a fire, but the Lord was not in the fire. And after the fire the sound of a low whisper.

1 Kings 19:12

Lord, quiet my heart so I can hear Your whisper. I have been looking for You in the loud places, but You are in the stillness. Teach me to listen with my heart. Nourish me quietly, steadily, deeply. Amen.

CHAPTER 46

You Are Fed by Grace

From the Gardener

I am the bread of life, beloved. Whoever comes to Me will never go hungry, and whoever believes in Me will never be thirsty. I am not a supplement. I am not a side dish. I am the main course—the sustenance your soul was made for, the nourishment nothing else can provide.

The world offers you a thousand substitutes. Quick fixes. Temporary satisfactions. Bread that fills your stomach for an hour and leaves you hungrier than before. But I am the bread that satisfies forever. One taste of My grace, and the deepest hunger of your heart begins to ease.

Come to My table, dear one. It is always set. There is always a place for you. And the bread I serve is not rationed or measured out in miserly portions. It is abundant, overflowing, more than you could ever consume. Eat, beloved. Eat until you are full.

Then Jesus declared, 'I am the bread of life. Whoever comes to me will never go hungry, and whoever believes in me will never be thirsty.'
John 6:35

Jesus, You are the bread of life. I have been filling myself with substitutes that leave me empty. Today I feast on You alone. Satisfy the deepest hunger of my heart with Your grace. You are enough. Amen.

CHAPTER 47

The Roots Go Deeper Than the Storm

From the Gardener

When the storm comes—and it will come, beloved—remember this: your roots go deeper than the wind can reach. The surface may shake. The branches may sway. The leaves may scatter in every direction. But the roots hold. They always hold, because they are anchored in Me.

Blessed is the one who trusts in the Lord. They are like a tree planted by the water that sends out its roots by the stream. It does not fear when heat comes; its leaves are always green. It has no worries in a year of drought and never fails to bear fruit.

The storm touches the surface, dear one. The roots are beyond its reach. And you are rooted in something—in Someone—who cannot be shaken, cannot be toppled, cannot be uprooted by any force in heaven or on earth.

Let the wind howl. Your roots are deep. You will stand.

But blessed is the one who trusts in the Lord, whose confidence is in him. They will be like a tree planted by the water that sends out its roots by the stream. It does not fear when heat comes; its leaves are always green.

Jeremiah 17:7–8

Father, send my roots deeper. Deeper than the storm can reach, deeper than fear can dig, deeper than doubt can burrow. Anchor me in You so firmly that no wind can move me. I trust You. Amen.

CHAPTER 48

Drink, Beloved

From the Gardener

Come, beloved. Come, all you who are thirsty. Come to the waters. You who have no money, come, buy and eat. Come, buy wine and milk without money and without cost. Why spend your labor on what does not satisfy? Listen to Me, and eat what is good, and you will delight in the richest of fare.

I am inviting you to drink—deeply, freely, without shame. Drink My love until it overflows. Drink My grace until it runs down your chin. Drink My peace until it fills every anxious corner of your mind. There is no limit. There is no meter running. There is no bill coming.

The world charges for everything. My love is free. The world rations its affection. My love is unlimited. The world gives with strings attached. My love comes with open hands and an open heart.

Drink, dear one. Drink until you cannot hold another drop. And then come back tomorrow and drink again.

Come, all you who are thirsty, come to the waters; and you who have no money, come, buy and eat! Come, buy wine and milk without money and without cost.

Isaiah 55:1

Lord, I am thirsty. I come to Your waters today—with empty hands and an empty cup. Fill me freely, generously, abundantly. I drink Your love. I drink Your grace. I drink until I overflow. Amen.

PART FIVE

Growing Strong

New life rising. Growth. Transformation. New leaves appearing. Reaching toward the light. Becoming something beautiful you never thought possible.

CHAPTER 49

The First Green Leaf

From the Gardener

Do you see it, beloved? Right there—at the tip of the branch that everyone said was dead. A tiny curl of green. The first new leaf. Proof that the graft took hold, that the sap is flowing, that life is returning to a place where death once reigned.

The winter is past. The rains are over and gone. Flowers appear on the earth, and the season of singing has come. I know the winter was long. I know you wondered if spring would ever arrive. But it has, dear one. It is here. And the first green leaf is the evidence.

Do not dismiss the small signs of life. Do not overlook the tiny shoot because you are waiting for the full-grown tree. This leaf is a miracle. This leaf is My promise kept. This leaf is the beginning of a growth so abundant it will take your breath away.

Look at what I am doing, beloved. It is starting. It has already started.

See! The winter is past; the rains are over and gone. Flowers appear on the earth; the season of singing has come, the cooing of doves is heard in our land.

Song of Solomon 2:11–12

Jesus, I see it—the first green leaf. New life is springing up in places I thought were dead. Thank You for the evidence of Your faithfulness. Thank You for spring after the longest winter. My heart is singing again. Amen.

CHAPTER 50

You Are Becoming

From the Gardener

Beloved, you look at yourself and you see all the things you are not yet. Not healed enough. Not whole enough. Not good enough. Not far enough along. You compare yourself to branches that have been grafted in longer, and you feel like a failure.

But I am not finished with you. The one who began a good work in you will carry it on to completion. You are not a finished product. You are a work in progress. And every day—even the hard ones, even the ones when you feel like you moved backward—I am still working. Still shaping. Still completing what I started.

Grace does not demand that you arrive instantly. Grace gives you permission to become. One day at a time. One choice at a time. One small step at a time. And I am with you in every step, celebrating every inch of progress, picking you up when you stumble, carrying you when you cannot walk.

You are becoming, dear one. And what you are becoming is beautiful.

"Being confident of this, that he who began a good work in you will carry it on to completion until the day of Christ Jesus."

Philippians 1:6

Father, thank You for not being finished with me. Thank You for the patience to let me become. I trust that You are completing what You started. Help me give myself the same grace You give me. Amen.

CHAPTER 51

Inch by Inch

From the Gardener

My child, growth is rarely dramatic. It does not happen in explosions or overnight transformations. It happens inch by inch, cell by cell, in the quiet places where no one is watching. Like a seed in the dark soil, pushing upward so slowly that no eye can track its movement—yet one morning, there it is, breaking through the surface into the light.

I know you wish the healing would come faster. I know you wish the transformation would hurry up. But I am not in a rush, dear one. I am doing something thorough, something deep, something that will last. Quick fixes produce quick results that quickly fade. What I am doing in you is meant to stand forever.

Do not despise the days of slow growth. Do not curse the seasons when it feels like nothing is happening. Beneath the surface, everything is happening. Roots are spreading. Strength is building. Life is gathering momentum. And when it finally breaks through the soil, it will be unstoppable.

He also said, 'This is what the kingdom of God is like. A man scatters seed on the ground. Night and day, whether he sleeps or gets up, the seed sprouts and grows, though he does not know how.'

Mark 4:26–28

Lord, give me patience for the slow growth. Help me trust the process even when I cannot see the progress. You are working beneath the surface, and I trust what You are building. Inch by inch, I am growing. Amen.

CHAPTER 52

Reaching for the Light

From the Gardener

Every living thing reaches for the light, beloved. It is instinct. It is design. The flower turns its face toward the sun without being told. The vine climbs the wall toward the brightness above. And you—you reach for Me, even when you do not realize you are doing it.

That longing in your heart? The one that aches for something more, something higher, something beyond what this world can offer? That is you reaching for the light. That is the part of you that was made for heaven, straining toward home.

One thing I ask of the Lord, and this is what I seek: to dwell in the house of the Lord all the days of my life, to gaze on the beauty of the Lord. That longing is not weakness, dear one. It is wisdom. It is the deepest part of you recognizing where life truly comes from.

Keep reaching, beloved. The Light is reaching back.

One thing I ask from the Lord, this only do I seek: that I may dwell in the house of the Lord all the days of my life, to gaze on the beauty of the Lord and to seek him in his temple.

Psalm 27:4

Jesus, You are the Light I am reaching for. Draw me closer. Turn my face toward You the way a flower turns toward the sun. I want to dwell in Your presence all the days of my life. Amen.

CHAPTER 53

The Old Bark Falls Away

From the Gardener

It is happening, beloved. Slowly, quietly, piece by piece—the old bark is falling away. The hard outer shell you built to protect yourself, the walls you constructed to keep people out, the armor you wore because vulnerability felt like suicide. It is loosening. It is peeling. It is dropping to the ground.

And I know that is terrifying. Without the armor, you feel exposed. Without the bark, the tender new wood underneath is vulnerable to every touch, every look, every word. But the new wood is strong, dear one. Stronger than the old bark ever was. Because it is alive, and what is alive can bend without breaking.

Put off the old self, which is being corrupted by its deceitful desires, and put on the new self, created to be like God in true righteousness and holiness. Let the old fall away. What is underneath is the real you—the you I have been growing all along.

You were taught, with regard to your former way of life, to put off your old self, which is being corrupted by its deceitful desires; to be made new in the attitude of your minds; and to put on the new self, created to be like God in true righteousness and holiness.

Ephesians 4:22–24

Father, I let the old bark fall. I release the walls, the armor, the masks. It is scary, but I trust that what You are uncovering is stronger and more beautiful than what I am letting go of. Clothe me in the new self You have created. Amen.

CHAPTER 54

I Am Making You New

From the Gardener

Behold, beloved. I am making all things new. Not patching. Not repairing. Not putting duct tape over the cracks and calling it fixed. I am making you *new*. New from the inside out. New at the cellular level. New in ways that will take eternity to fully reveal.

This is not renovation. This is resurrection. I do not take the old version of you and improve it. I speak a word and the old passes away, and from the same breath, the new is born. Fresh. Clean. Unstained by the past. Unmarked by the failures. Free.

You do not have to carry the weight of who you used to be. That person has been laid to rest. The person standing in their place—reading these words, breathing this air, living this moment—is new. Brand new. And I am not finished yet.

I am making you new, dear one. Can you feel it?

He who was seated on the throne said, 'I am making everything new!' Then he said, 'Write this down, for these words are trustworthy and true.'

Revelation 21:5

Lord, make me new. Not patched, not repaired—new. I lay down the old and I receive the new creation You are forming in me. Your words are trustworthy and true. I believe them. Amen.

CHAPTER 55

Taller Than You Know

From the Gardener

You have grown, beloved. More than you realize. You are so busy looking at how far you still have to go that you have not turned around to see how far you have already come. But I have been watching, and I can tell you: you are taller than you know.

The prayers you could not pray six months ago—you pray them now without thinking. The temptations that used to flatten you—you walk past them now with barely a glance. The fears that once controlled your every move—you face them now with a quiet courage that takes My breath away.

Those who hope in the Lord will renew their strength. They will soar on wings like eagles. They will run and not grow weary. They will walk and not be faint. That is you, dear one. That is you right now, even if you cannot see it.

Turn around and look at the view, beloved. You have climbed higher than you think.

But those who hope in the Lord will renew their strength. They will soar on wings like eagles; they will run and not grow weary, they will walk and not be faint.

Isaiah 40:31

Jesus, help me see the growth You see. I have been so focused on how far I have to go that I have forgotten how far I have come. Thank You for renewing my strength. I am taller than I know. Amen.

CHAPTER 56

The Rings of Your Story

From the Gardener

Have you ever seen the cross-section of a great old tree, beloved? Each ring tells the story of a year—a wide ring for a year of rain and plenty, a thin ring for a year of drought and struggle. But every ring, whether wide or thin, added strength. Every season, whether easy or hard, made the tree stronger.

Your story is written in rings, too. Each year of your life—the good ones and the terrible ones, the years of abundance and the years of barely surviving—has added a ring of strength to your soul. Nothing was wasted. Nothing was meaningless. Every season shaped you.

Teach us to number our days, that we may gain a heart of wisdom. Your days are numbered, dear one, and every one of them counts. Every one of them has been recorded in My book. Every one of them has been used to make you who you are today.

Your rings are beautiful, beloved. Every single one.

Teach us to number our days, that we may gain a heart of wisdom.

Psalm 90:12

Father, thank You for every ring of my story—the wide ones and the thin ones. Give me a heart of wisdom to see that every season has made me stronger. My story is not wasted. It is written by You. Amen.

CHAPTER 57

Do Not Despise Small Beginnings

From the Gardener

The world celebrates the spectacular, beloved. The grand entrances. The overnight successes. The explosive transformations that make headlines. And when your growth is quiet and small and incremental, the world yawns and looks away.

But I am not the world. I do not despise small beginnings. I delight in them. Because I know what a mustard seed becomes. I know what a tiny ember can do. I know that the mightiest oak was once an acorn so small a child could hold it in their palm.

Your beginning may look small to others. Your progress may seem insignificant to those who are not paying attention. But I am paying attention, and I am rejoicing. Because every small beginning is a seed of something great, and I am the God who specializes in growing great things from small seeds.

Do not despise the smallness, dear one. It is the birthplace of something mighty.

Who dares despise the day of small things, since the seven eyes of the Lord that range throughout the earth will rejoice when they see the chosen capstone in the hand of Zerubbabel?

Zechariah 4:10

Lord, I choose not to despise my small beginnings. I trust that You see the mighty oak inside the tiny acorn. Grow something great from my small start. I believe in Your power over my smallness. Amen.

CHAPTER 58

Rooted and Established

From the Gardener

You are no longer a branch teetering on the edge of the graft, beloved. The wood has fused. The sap flows freely. You are rooted and established in love—a love so wide and long and high and deep that it will take eternity to explore it all.

I pray that you, being rooted and established in love, may have power, together with all the Lord's holy people, to grasp how wide and long and high and deep is the love of Christ, and to know this love that surpasses knowledge. This is My prayer for you, dear one. Not that you would know about My love, but that you would *know* My love. Experience it. Feel it in your bones. Let it become the ground you walk on.

You are not rootless anymore. You are not drifting. You are anchored in something eternal, something unshakeable, something that will hold you when everything else gives way.

You are rooted, beloved. Deeply, firmly, permanently rooted.

And I pray that you, being rooted and established in love, may have power, together with all the Lord's holy people, to grasp how wide and long and high and deep is the love of Christ, and to know this love that surpasses knowledge.

Ephesians 3:17–19

Father, root me deeper in Your love. Not just knowledge of it, but experience of it. Let me grasp how wide and long and high and deep it truly is. I want to know Your love in my bones. Amen.

CHAPTER 59

You Are Not What You Were

From the Gardener

The accuser loves to remind you of what you were, beloved. He pulls out the old photographs and waves them in your face. *Remember this? Remember who you used to be? You have not really changed. You are still that person.*

But the accuser is a liar. You are not what you were. You were washed. You were sanctified. You were justified in the name of the Lord Jesus Christ and by the Spirit of our God. The person in those old photographs? They have been laid to rest. Buried with Christ in baptism. Raised to new life.

When the enemy shows you the old pictures, show him the empty tomb. Remind him that the God you serve is in the business of resurrection. What was dead is alive. What was lost is found. What was broken is whole. And what you were is not what you are.

You are new, dear one. Hold your head high.

And that is what some of you were. But you were washed, you were sanctified, you were justified in the name of the Lord Jesus Christ and by the Spirit of our God.

1 Corinthians 6:11

Jesus, I am not what I was. I have been washed, sanctified, and justified. When the accuser reminds me of my past, I will remind him of Your cross. I am new. I walk in newness of life. Amen.

CHAPTER 60

Watch What I Will Do

From the Gardener

Beloved, you have not even begun to see what I have planned for you. The growth so far? It is just the first chapter. The healing? It is just the opening note of a symphony. The transformation? You are still in the prologue. The best is yet to come.

I am able to do immeasurably more than all you ask or imagine, according to My power that is at work within you. Immeasurably more. Not slightly more. Not a little more. More than your wildest, most audacious, most outrageous prayer could ever conceive.

So dream bigger, dear one. Pray bolder. Hope harder. Because the God who grafted a wild branch into a living tree is the same God who can do anything, and He is not finished surprising you yet.

Watch what I will do, beloved. Just watch.

Now to him who is able to do immeasurably more than all we ask or imagine, according to his power that is at work within us, to him be glory in the church and in Christ Jesus throughout all generations, for ever and ever! Amen.

Ephesians 3:20–21

Lord, I am watching. I am waiting. I am expecting immeasurably more than I could ever ask or imagine. Surprise me with Your goodness. Astonish me with Your power. I believe You have more in store. Amen.

PART SIX

The Pruning

The painful but necessary pruning. God's loving discipline. Being shaped, refined, cut back so you can bear more fruit. The Gardener's careful hands.

CHAPTER 61

Every Branch He Prunes

From the Gardener

Beloved, the pruning is not a sign of My displeasure. It is a sign of My investment. I do not prune branches I have given up on. I prune the ones that bear fruit so they will bear even more. The very fact that the shears have touched you is proof that you are fruitful, not failing.

I know it hurts. I know it feels like loss. I know you look at the pieces on the ground—the things I have cut away—and you grieve. But what I remove is never the best of you. It is the excess, the distraction, the growth that was draining your energy without producing anything eternal.

Trust the Gardener, dear one. Every cut is calculated. Every snip is strategic. I am not careless with you. I am precise. I am intentional. And when the pruning is done, you will bear more fruit than you ever thought possible.

He cuts off every branch in me that bears no fruit, while every branch that does bear fruit he prunes so that it will be even more fruitful.

John 15:2

Lord, I trust the pruning. Even though it hurts, I believe it is for my good. Cut away what is draining me. Remove what is distracting me. Shape me to bear more fruit for Your glory. Amen.

CHAPTER 62

This Will Not Destroy You

From the Gardener

My child, I know what it looks like. I know it looks like the end. The enemy has aimed his best weapon at you, and every fiber of your being is screaming that this is the blow that will finish you off. But I am telling you right now: this will not destroy you.

No weapon formed against you shall prosper. Not this one. Not any one. Not ever. The weapons will form—I never said they would not. The attacks will come. The storms will rage. The enemy will try. But he will not succeed. Because you are Mine, and what is Mine is protected by the power of the Almighty.

You will come through this. Not barely. Not hanging by a thread. You will come through this standing, breathing, stronger than when it started. Because I am the God who turns weapons into plowshares and trials into testimonies.

This will not destroy you, beloved. I will not allow it.

No weapon forged against you will prevail, and you will refute every tongue that accuses you. This is the heritage of the servants of the Lord, and this is their vindication from me," declares the Lord.

Isaiah 54:17

Father, I declare over my life today: no weapon formed against me will prosper. This trial will not destroy me. I am protected by Your power and covered by Your love. I will come through. Amen.

CHAPTER 63

I Am the Gardener, Not the Storm

From the Gardener

Dear one, I need to clear something up. When the storm hits and the pain comes and the ground shakes beneath your feet, your first instinct is to look at the sky and ask, *Why are You doing this to me?* But I am not the storm. I am the Gardener.

I am not the one sending the devastation. I am the one walking through it with you, sheltering you under My branches, holding you steady while the wind howls. The Lord is good, a refuge in times of trouble. He cares for those who trust in Him. That is who I am. I am your refuge, not your affliction.

The enemy brings destruction. The world brings chaos. But I bring refuge. I bring protection. I bring the steady hands of a Gardener who tends His branches even in the midst of the worst storm.

Do not confuse Me with the storm, beloved. I am the shelter from it.

The Lord is good, a refuge in times of trouble. He cares for those who trust in him.

Nahum 1:7

Lord, forgive me for blaming You for the storm. You are not my affliction—You are my refuge. I run to You today, not away from You. You are good, and You care for me. I trust You. Amen.

CHAPTER 64

The Shape of Grace

From the Gardener

I am shaping you, beloved. Like a potter at the wheel, I am pressing and molding and forming you into something beautiful. I know it does not feel beautiful right now. Right now it feels like pressure and heat and a relentless spinning that will not stop. But the potter sees what the clay cannot.

Can I not do with you as this potter does? Like clay in the hand of the potter, so are you in My hand. I am not being rough with you. I am being intentional. Every press of My thumb, every turn of the wheel, every moment of shaping is done with love and purpose.

The shape I am giving you is the shape of grace. It is a shape that can hold the love I want to pour into you. It is a shape that can carry the purpose I have designed for you. And when the shaping is done, you will be a vessel of honor—beautiful, useful, filled to the brim with glory.

He said, 'Can I not do with you, Israel, as this potter does?' declares the Lord. 'Like clay in the hand of the potter, so are you in my hand.'

Jeremiah 18:6

Father, I am clay in Your hands. Shape me into the vessel You have designed. I surrender to the pressure, the heat, the spinning—because I trust the Potter. Make me beautiful. Make me useful. Make me Yours. Amen.

CHAPTER 65

Pain with Purpose

From the Gardener

I will not lie to you, beloved. The road of faith includes pain. But it is never meaningless pain. It is never random, pointless suffering that leads nowhere. Every trial you face has been filtered through My hands, and each one carries a purpose—even when the purpose is hidden from your eyes.

Consider it pure joy when you face trials of many kinds, because you know that the testing of your faith produces perseverance. And perseverance produces character. And character produces hope. And hope does not put you to shame. Every link in that chain matters, dear one. Every stage of the process is producing something eternal in you.

The pain is real. I will never dismiss it. But so is the purpose. And one day, when you stand on the other side of this trial and look back, you will see what I was building in the furnace. And you will weep—not with grief, but with gratitude.

Consider it pure joy, my brothers and sisters, whenever you face trials of many kinds, because you know that the testing of your faith produces perseverance. Let perseverance finish its work so that you may be mature and complete, not lacking anything.

James 1:2–4

Lord, I believe the pain has purpose, even when I cannot see it. Produce perseverance in me. Build character. Grow hope. Let this trial make me mature and complete, lacking nothing. Amen.

CHAPTER 66

I Hold the Shears

From the Gardener

The shears are in My hands, beloved—not in the hands of the enemy. I am the one who decides what stays and what goes. I am the one who knows which branch is excess and which is essential. The enemy would hack you to pieces, but I am precise. I am surgical. I am careful.

As a father has compassion on his children, so I have compassion on you. I know how you are formed. I remember that you are dust. I do not push you beyond what you can bear. I do not cut deeper than is necessary. I hold the shears with the same hands that hold you—hands of compassion, hands of mercy, hands that would sooner bleed than harm you unnecessarily.

Do not be afraid of the pruning, dear one. Be afraid of a life that was never tended. The fact that I hold the shears means I am invested in your growth. And I am the gentlest Gardener you will ever know.

As a father has compassion on his children, so the Lord has compassion on those who fear him; for he knows how we are formed, he remembers that we are dust.

Psalm 103:13–14

Father, thank You for holding the shears with compassion. You know how I am formed. You remember that I am dust. I trust Your gentle precision. Prune me with love. Amen.

CHAPTER 67

What I Remove, I Replace

From the Gardener

Beloved, I never leave an empty space unfilled. When I remove something from your life, it is because I have something better to put in its place. I do not strip you bare and walk away. I strip you bare and clothe you in something new—something richer, stronger, more beautiful than what was there before.

I will repay you for the years the locusts have eaten. Every year the enemy stole from you, I will restore. Every joy he devoured, I will replace. Every harvest he destroyed, I will replant. I am not a God of deficit. I am a God of restoration, and My restoration is always greater than the original.

Do not mourn what I have removed, dear one. Make room for what I am about to provide. The replacement is already on its way, and when it arrives, you will forget what was taken. The new will eclipse the old so completely that you will wonder why you ever held on so tightly.

I will repay you for the years the locusts have eaten—the great locust and the young locust, the other locusts and the locust swarm—my great army that I sent among you.

Joel 2:25

Lord, I trust that what You remove, You replace with something better. Restore the years the locusts have eaten. Fill every empty space with Your abundance. I make room for the new. Amen.

CHAPTER 68

Do Not Fear the Cutting Back

From the Gardener

My child, I know the pruning season feels like the valley of the shadow of death. The cutting back feels like dying. But even in this valley—especially in this valley—I am with you. My rod and My staff, they comfort you. The rod to protect you from the predators that prowl in the dark. The staff to guide you through the narrow places.

You do not need to fear the cutting back. Fear would have you believe that what is being removed is essential, that you cannot survive without it. But fear is a liar, beloved. What I am removing was weighing you down. What I am cutting away was stealing your energy, your joy, your fruitfulness.

After the pruning, the branch does not shrink. It explodes with new growth. The energy that was being wasted on excess is redirected into fruit. And the fruit that comes after the pruning is always the sweetest, the richest, the most abundant.

Do not fear the cutting back, dear one. Fear the staying the same.

Even though I walk through the darkest valley, I will fear no evil, for you are with me; your rod and your staff, they comfort me.

Psalm 23:4

Lord, I will not fear the valley. Your rod and Your staff comfort me. I trust that the cutting back will lead to the greatest growth I have ever known. Walk with me through the dark places. Amen.

CHAPTER 69

Less of You, More of Me

From the Gardener

Beloved, the pruning is not just about removing the bad. Sometimes it is about making room for the better. Less of your anxiety, more of My peace. Less of your striving, more of My rest. Less of your control, more of My sovereignty. Less of you, more of Me.

He must become greater; I must become less. This is not a punishment. It is a promotion. When you decrease, you are not diminished. You are expanded—because the space you make is filled with the infinite God of the universe. There is no trade in all of history more favorable than this: giving up the limited for the unlimited, the temporary for the eternal, the human for the divine.

Let Me increase in your life, dear one. Let My voice grow louder and yours grow softer. Let My will overshadow yours. Not because you do not matter, but because when I fill you, you become more yourself than you have ever been.

He must become greater; I must become less.

John 3:30

Jesus, more of You, less of me. Increase in my life until You fill every corner. I surrender my control, my striving, my anxiety. Fill me with Your peace, Your rest, Your sovereignty. Amen.

CHAPTER 70

Refined Like Silver

From the Gardener

Do you know how a silversmith refines silver, beloved? He sits before the fire, watching the metal melt, keeping his eyes fixed on it the entire time. He cannot look away—not even for a moment—because if the silver stays in the fire one second too long, it will be ruined. And he knows the silver is ready when he can see his own reflection in it.

That is what I am doing with you. I am sitting before the fire, watching you with unwavering attention, waiting for the impurities to rise to the surface so I can skim them away. I will not leave you in the fire one moment longer than necessary. And I will know you are ready when I look at you and see My own reflection looking back.

The fire is hot, dear one. I will not pretend otherwise. But the Refiner is present, and He will not look away.

He will sit as a refiner and purifier of silver; he will purify the Levites and refine them like gold and silver.

Malachi 3:3

Lord, I trust You at the fire. You are watching. You will not leave me in the flames one moment too long. Refine me until You see Your reflection in me. I submit to the process. Amen.

CHAPTER 71

The Tenderness After the Cut

From the Gardener

After the pruning, beloved, comes the tenderness. I do not cut and walk away. I cut and then I tend. I bind the wound. I cover it with balm. I wrap it with care. I stay beside you, watching for infection, protecting the tender place from further harm.

Come, let us return to the Lord. He has torn us to pieces but He will heal us; He has injured but He will bind up our wounds. After two days He will revive us; on the third day He will restore us, that we may live in His presence. The tearing is not the end, dear one. The healing always follows.

I am gentle with you in the aftermath. I speak softly. I move slowly. I give you time to recover, time to breathe, time to let the wound close. I am not in a hurry to prune again. I am patient. I am tender. And I am right here.

Come, let us return to the Lord. He has torn us to pieces but he will heal us; he has injured us but he will bind up our wounds.

Hosea 6:1

Father, thank You for the tenderness after the cut. Thank You for binding my wounds, for staying close, for being gentle with me in the aftermath. Heal me, Lord. Restore me. I trust Your gentle hands. Amen.

CHAPTER 72

You Will Bloom Again

From the Gardener

Beloved, I know you look at yourself after the pruning and you see bare branches. Stripped. Empty. Cut back to almost nothing. And you wonder if you will ever bloom again. If there is enough left of you to produce anything beautiful.

But there is hope for a tree. If it is cut down, it will sprout again, and its new shoots will not fail. At the scent of water it will bud and put forth shoots like a plant. At the first scent of My presence, at the first drop of My living water, the buds will come. And from the buds, the blooms. And from the blooms, the fruit.

You will bloom again, dear one. Not in spite of the pruning, but because of it. The pruning made room for the most spectacular blooming season of your life. It is coming. It is close. And when it arrives, you will be covered in blossoms so thick they will hide every scar.

You will bloom again, beloved. I promise.

At least there is hope for a tree: If it is cut down, it will sprout again, and its new shoots will not fail. At the scent of water it will bud and put forth shoots like a plant.

Job 14:7–9

Lord, I believe I will bloom again. Pour Your water over my bare branches. Let the buds come, the blossoms open, the fruit appear. I trust that my best blooming season is ahead of me. Amen.

PART SEVEN

Bearing Fruit

Your life producing something beautiful. Fruit of the Spirit. Your pain becoming someone else's comfort. The harvest God always intended.

CHAPTER 73

The Fruit I Always Intended

From the Gardener

This, beloved—this is why I grafted you in. Not just so you could be saved, but so you could be fruitful. Not just so you could survive, but so you could thrive. Not just so you could receive life, but so you could give it away. This is My Father's glory: that you bear much fruit, showing yourselves to be My disciples.

The fruit was always the plan. From the moment I first saw you growing wild on the hillside, I imagined the harvest your life would produce. Love. Joy. Peace. Patience. Kindness. Goodness. Faithfulness. Gentleness. Self-control. These are the fruits that grow on the branches of those who are grafted into Me.

You are bearing fruit right now, dear one, even if you cannot see it. Every act of love, every moment of patience, every choice to be kind when it costs you something—that is fruit. And I am gathering it with joy.

This is to my Father's glory, that you bear much fruit, showing yourselves to be my disciples.

John 15:8

Father, let my life bear the fruit You always intended. Love, joy, peace, patience, kindness, goodness, faithfulness, gentleness, self-control—let them grow in abundance on the branch You grafted in. For Your glory. Amen.

CHAPTER 74

Love Is the First Fruit

From the Gardener

Of all the fruit your life will bear, beloved, love is the first and the greatest. Not the sentimental kind. Not the kind that evaporates when things get hard. But the kind that is patient when every nerve in your body is screaming to snap. The kind that is kind when kindness costs you something. The kind that does not keep score.

Love is not a feeling, dear one. It is a decision. A daily, stubborn, sometimes exhausting decision to keep choosing the other person's good over your own comfort. It does not envy. It does not boast. It is not proud. It always protects, always trusts, always hopes, always perseveres.

And here is the secret: you cannot produce this love on your own. It flows through you from the root. It is My love, expressed through your hands, your words, your life. You are the branch. I am the source. And when My love flows through you, it changes everything it touches.

Love is patient, love is kind. It does not envy, it does not boast, it is not proud. It does not dishonor others, it is not self-seeking, it is not easily angered, it keeps no record of wrongs.

1 Corinthians 13:4–5

Lord, let Your love flow through me. Not my love—Yours. Patient when I want to snap. Kind when it costs me. Let me be a channel of the love that comes from the root. Amen.

CHAPTER 75

Joy from Ashes

From the Gardener

I am giving you beauty for ashes, beloved. The oil of joy instead of mourning. A garment of praise instead of a spirit of despair. The very places where you wept the hardest are becoming the places where joy blooms the brightest.

This joy is not the world's joy. The world's joy is fragile—it depends on circumstances, on outcomes, on everything going according to plan. My joy is unshakeable. It is rooted in something deeper than your situation. It is rooted in Me, and I do not change.

The joy that comes from ashes is the most precious kind. It is a joy that has been tested by fire and survived. It is a joy that knows the taste of tears and chooses to sing anyway. It is a defiant, beautiful, holy joy that the enemy cannot steal because he did not give it and he cannot take it away.

Let the joy come, dear one. You have earned these ashes. Let Me turn them into beauty.

...to bestow on them a crown of beauty instead of ashes, the oil of joy instead of mourning, and a garment of praise instead of a spirit of despair.

Isaiah 61:3

Jesus, take my ashes and give me beauty. Take my mourning and give me joy. Take my despair and clothe me in praise. I receive the exchange of Your grace today. Amen.

CHAPTER 76

Peace That Passes Understanding

From the Gardener

Beloved, I am giving you a peace that the world cannot give and the world cannot take away. A peace that does not make logical sense. A peace that settles over your heart even when the circumstances around you are screaming that you should be terrified.

Do not be anxious about anything, dear one. Instead, in every situation, by prayer and petition, with thanksgiving, present your requests to Me. And My peace—the peace that transcends all understanding—will guard your heart and your mind.

This peace is not the absence of trouble. It is My presence in the middle of trouble. It is the calm at the center of the hurricane, the stillness at the bottom of the ocean while the waves rage on the surface. It is knowing—truly knowing, in the marrow of your bones—that I am in control even when everything looks out of control.

Breathe, beloved. My peace is here. Let it guard your heart.

And the peace of God, which transcends all understanding, will guard your hearts and your minds in Christ Jesus.

Philippians 4:7

Father, I present my anxieties to You right now. Every worry, every fear, every racing thought. Replace them with Your peace—the peace that passes understanding. Guard my heart. Guard my mind. Amen.

CHAPTER 77

Patient in the Waiting

From the Gardener

My child, I know the waiting is hard. You have been standing in faith for so long, believing for the breakthrough, hoping for the answer, and it has not come yet. Your arms are tired from holding on. Your heart is weary from hoping.

But patience is a fruit, not a punishment. It is something beautiful growing in you while you wait. Every day that you choose to keep believing, to keep hoping, to keep trusting when you have every reason to quit—that is fruit. That is faith made visible. That is the kind of character that can only be forged in the furnace of delay.

Be joyful in hope, patient in affliction, faithful in prayer. The answer is coming, beloved. The breakthrough is on its way. But while you wait, do not miss the fruit that is growing in the waiting. Some of the sweetest fruit of your life will have been harvested from these patient, persistent, prayerful days.

Be **joyful in hope, patient in affliction, faithful in prayer.**

Romans 12:12

Lord, give me patience for the waiting. Help me be joyful in hope and faithful in prayer while I wait for Your answer. Let the waiting produce beautiful fruit in my life. Amen.

CHAPTER 78

Your Kindness Changes the World

From the Gardener

You underestimate the power of your kindness, beloved. You think it is small—a smile, a gentle word, a moment of patience with someone who does not deserve it. But kindness is not small. It is seismic. One act of kindness creates a ripple that spreads outward in ways you will never see this side of heaven.

The cashier who was barely holding it together until you looked her in the eye and thanked her by name. The neighbor who was one bad day from giving up until you brought over that plate of cookies. The stranger who was invisible until you held the door. You changed something in them, dear one. You may have saved something in them.

Your kindness is My love with skin on. It is the fruit of being grafted into the tree of life. And it changes the world—one small, holy, seemingly insignificant act at a time.

Those who are kind benefit themselves, but the cruel bring ruin on themselves.

Proverbs 11:17

Jesus, make me kind. Not just nice, but genuinely, sacrificially kind. Open my eyes to the people around me who need a ripple of Your love today. Let my kindness change someone's world. Amen.

CHAPTER 79

Goodness Poured Out

From the Gardener

Beloved, I have set a table before you in the presence of your enemies. I have anointed your head with oil. Your cup overflows. Not half-full, not adequate, not just enough to get by—overflowing. Spilling over the edges. Running down the sides. Too much to contain.

That is how I give. Abundantly. Extravagantly. With a generosity that embarrasses the stingy and astonishes the skeptical. My goodness is not rationed. It is poured out—pressed down, shaken together, running over—into your lap.

And when your cup overflows, it spills onto everyone around you. Your goodness—the goodness that flows from being grafted into Me—touches everyone you encounter. Your family. Your friends. Your colleagues. The stranger at the gas station. They all get wet when your cup runs over.

Let the goodness pour, dear one. There is always more where that came from.

You prepare a table before me in the presence of my enemies. You anoint my head with oil; my cup overflows. Surely your goodness and love will follow me all the days of my life, and I will dwell in the house of the Lord forever.

Psalm 23:5–6

Father, let my cup overflow with Your goodness. Let it spill onto everyone around me. Let Your goodness and love follow me all the days of my life. I receive the abundance You pour out. Amen.

CHAPTER 80

Faithful When No One Sees

From the Gardener

I see you, beloved. In the quiet moments when no audience applauds and no camera records, I see you. I see the faithfulness that no one else notices. The prayer you whispered in the dark. The temptation you resisted when giving in would have been so easy. The right thing you did when the wrong thing was more convenient.

Whoever can be trusted with very little can also be trusted with much. And you have been faithful in the little things, dear one. Faithful in the unsexy, unglamorous, unnoticed acts of daily obedience that build the foundation of a life that lasts.

The world rewards the spectacular. I reward the faithful. And your faithfulness—quiet, consistent, unwavering—is building something that will stand when the spectacular has crumbled to dust.

Keep being faithful, beloved. I am watching. And I am smiling.

Whoever can be trusted with very little can also be trusted with much, and whoever is dishonest with very little will also be dishonest with much.

Luke 16:10

Lord, help me be faithful in the little things—the unseen, unnoticed, unrewarded acts of obedience. You see what no one else sees. I do this for You, and Your approval is enough. Amen.

CHAPTER 81

Gentle Strength

From the Gardener

The world tells you that gentleness is weakness, beloved. That to be soft is to be vulnerable. That you must armor yourself, harden yourself, close yourself off to survive. But I am telling you the opposite: gentleness is the greatest strength you will ever possess.

Take My yoke upon you and learn from Me, for I am gentle and humble in heart, and you will find rest for your souls. I am gentle—and I hold the universe in My hands. I am humble—and I sit on the throne of heaven. Gentleness is not the absence of power. It is power under control. It is the lion choosing to lie down with the lamb.

Be gentle with the people around you, dear one. Be gentle with yourself. You have been through so much. You do not need more harshness. You need the gentle strength that comes from knowing you are loved, knowing you are safe, knowing you are held by the gentlest hands in the universe.

Take my yoke upon you and learn from me, for I am gentle and humble in heart, and you will find rest for your souls.

Matthew 11:29

Jesus, teach me Your gentleness. Not weakness, but power under control. Help me be gentle with others and with myself. I take Your yoke. I learn from You. I find rest. Amen.

CHAPTER 82

The Discipline of Abiding

From the Gardener

Remain in Me, beloved, and I will remain in you. No branch can bear fruit by itself; it must remain in the vine. Neither can you bear fruit unless you remain in Me. This is the great discipline of the grafted life: not striving, not performing, not achieving—but remaining. Abiding. Staying connected.

Self-control is not gritting your teeth and white-knuckling your way through another day. Self-control is choosing, moment by moment, to stay attached to the vine. To remain in My word. To remain in My presence. To remain in My love. Because when you remain in Me, the fruit comes naturally. You do not have to manufacture it. It grows on its own.

The branch that remains bears fruit. The branch that disconnects withers. It is that simple, dear one. Stay connected. Stay close. Stay with Me.

Abide, beloved. That is all I ask. Just abide.

Remain in me, as I also remain in you. No branch can bear fruit by itself; it must remain in the vine. Neither can you bear fruit unless you remain in me. I am the vine; you are the branches.

John 15:4–5

Lord, I choose to remain. To abide. To stay connected to You every moment of every day. I do not want to strive—I want to abide. Keep me close, Jesus. I remain in You. Amen.

CHAPTER 83

Your Scars Bear Witness

From the Gardener

Beloved, do not hide your scars. They are not marks of shame. They are marks of survival. They are the places where My healing power was put on display. And they are the very things that will make your testimony believable to someone who is still in the fire.

The God of all comfort comforts you in all your troubles so that you can comfort those in any trouble with the comfort you yourself received from God. Your pain has a purpose beyond your own healing. It has equipped you to sit beside someone who is breaking apart and say, with authority, "I know how this feels. And I know the God who brought me through it."

Your scars are your credentials, dear one. They prove that you have been in the battle and come out the other side. They prove that the graft holds, that the root sustains, that the Gardener is faithful. Do not hide them. Show them. And watch what God does through your wounds.

Praise be to the God and Father of our Lord Jesus Christ, the Father of compassion and the God of all comfort, who comforts us in all our troubles, so that we can comfort those in any trouble with the comfort we ourselves receive from God.

2 Corinthians 1:3–4

Father, use my scars. Let my pain become someone else's comfort. Let my story become someone else's hope. I do not hide what You have healed. I share it for Your glory. Amen.

CHAPTER 84

A Harvest You Cannot Count

From the Gardener

Do not grow weary, beloved. Do not give up. I know the sowing has been hard. I know you have planted seeds in tears, watered them with prayers, and wondered if anything would ever come up. But the harvest is coming. And it will be so abundant you will not be able to count it.

Let us not become weary in doing good, for at the proper time we will reap a harvest if we do not give up. At the proper time—not your time, not the world's time, but the perfect, divinely appointed time—the seeds you have sown will break through the soil and produce a harvest beyond your wildest dreams.

Every prayer you prayed that felt like it disappeared into silence—it is a seed. Every act of kindness that went unnoticed—it is a seed. Every tear you cried over someone you love—it is a seed. And harvest time is coming, dear one. Hold on. Do not give up. The reaping is near.

Let us not become weary in doing good, for at the proper time we will reap a harvest if we do not give up.

Galatians 6:9

Lord, I will not grow weary. I will not give up. I trust that the harvest is coming at the proper time. Give me strength to keep sowing, keep praying, keep believing. The reaping is near. Amen.

PART EIGHT

Weathering the Storms

Storms will come. Winds will blow. But because you are grafted into something stronger than yourself, you will not be torn away. Standing firm in the tempest.

CHAPTER 85

The Storm Does Not Define You

From the Gardener

Beloved, you are not your storm. The diagnosis does not define you. The divorce does not define you. The bankruptcy, the betrayal, the loss—none of it defines you. You are defined by whose you are, not by what happened to you.

In all these things, you are more than a conqueror through Him who loved you. More than a conqueror. Not barely surviving. Not hanging on by a thread. Triumphant. Victorious. Overcoming. Not because of your own strength, but because of Mine.

The storm is a chapter in your story, not the title of your book. And the Author who is writing your story has already penned the ending—and I promise you, beloved, it is a good one.

No, in all these things we are more than conquerors through him who loved us.

Romans 8:37

Lord, I am not my storm. I am more than a conqueror through You. Remind me today that no circumstance has the power to define me. Only Your love defines me. Amen.

CHAPTER 86

I Am Your Shelter

From the Gardener

Come to Me, dear one. Come under the shadow of My wings. Whoever dwells in the shelter of the Most High will rest in the shadow of the Almighty. I am your shelter—not a flimsy tent, but a fortress. Not a temporary covering, but an eternal refuge.

I will say of the Lord, "He is my refuge and my fortress, my God, in whom I trust." This is your declaration, beloved. This is the truth you speak over your life when the sky grows dark and the thunder begins to roll. Not "I hope He will protect me," but "He *is* my refuge." Present tense. Right now. Already.

Run to Me, dear one. Not away from the storm—to Me. I am closer than the storm. I am bigger than the storm. And I am not going anywhere.

Whoever dwells in the shelter of the Most High will rest in the shadow of the Almighty. I will say of the Lord, 'He is my refuge and my fortress, my God, in whom I trust.'

Psalm 91:1–2

Father, You are my refuge and my fortress. I run to You today. Hide me under the shadow of Your wings. I trust You completely. Amen.

CHAPTER 87

Winds Will Blow

From the Gardener

I never promised you a life without storms, beloved. The rain will fall, the streams will rise, the winds will blow and beat against your house. But I did promise this: if you build your life on Me, on the rock of My words, your house will stand. It will not fall.

The storms are not a sign of My absence. They are a test of your foundation. And your foundation is solid, dear one. It is built on the rock—on My truth, My love, My promises. The winds can howl all they want. The rock does not move.

You will weather this storm, beloved. And when it passes, you will still be standing—not because you were strong, but because what you are standing on is unshakeable.

Therefore everyone who hears these words of mine and puts them into practice is like a wise man who built his house on the rock. The rain came down, the streams rose, and the winds blew and beat against that house; yet it did not fall, because it had its foundation on the rock.

Matthew 7:24–25

Jesus, my life is built on You—the rock. When the winds blow, I will not be shaken. Help me stand firm on the foundation of Your truth. Amen

CHAPTER 88

Bend but Do Not Break

From the Gardener

A rigid branch snaps in the wind, beloved. But a flexible one—one that has been made supple by the sap flowing through it—that one bends. It sways. It yields to the force of the storm without surrendering to it. And when the wind stops, it springs back, stronger than before.

I am making you resilient, dear one. Not hard. Not brittle. Resilient. It is God who arms you with strength and keeps your way secure. He makes your feet like the feet of a deer and causes you to stand on the heights. Not rigid feet, but sure feet. Nimble feet. Feet that can navigate the rocky places without stumbling.

Bend, beloved. Yield. Let the storm move through you without breaking you. You are more flexible than you know, because the sap of My Spirit has made you supple. You will bend, but you will not break.

It is God who arms me with strength and keeps my way secure. He makes my feet like the feet of a deer; he causes me to stand on the heights.

Psalm 18:32–33

Lord, make me resilient. Not rigid, not brittle, but flexible and strong. Help me bend without breaking, yield without surrendering, and spring back stronger. Amen.

CHAPTER 89

I Will Calm Your Sea

From the Gardener

The waves are high, beloved. I know. The boat feels like it is going under. You are bailing water as fast as you can, and it is not enough. You look around and wonder where I am, and part of you is terrified that I am asleep—or worse, that I do not care.

But I am here. And with a word, I can calm your sea. Peace, be still. That is all it takes—one word from My mouth, and the wind dies, the waves flatten, the chaos surrenders. I am not frantic in your storm, dear one. I am sovereign over it.

I may not always calm the storm when you want Me to. Sometimes I calm it instantly. Sometimes I calm you instead, giving you supernatural peace in the middle of the gale. But either way, you will not go under. The boat will not sink. Because I am in it with you.

He got up, rebuked the wind and said to the waves, 'Quiet! Be still!' Then the wind died down and it was completely calm.

Mark 4:39

Jesus, speak peace over my storm. Quiet the wind. Still the waves. And if the storm continues, calm my heart in the middle of it. You are in the boat with me. I will not go under. Amen.

CHAPTER 90

The Anchor Holds

From the Gardener

Beloved, you do not need to navigate the storm alone. You have an anchor—firm, secure, unbreakable. An anchor for the soul that reaches past the waves, past the depths, past the shifting sands, all the way into the throne room of heaven.

We have this hope as an anchor for the soul, firm and secure. When everything around you is shifting, when the ground feels like it is moving, when nothing seems stable or certain—the anchor holds. Not because you are gripping it tightly, but because it is embedded in the bedrock of God's faithfulness.

Let the waves come, dear one. Let the wind rage. Let the boat rock. The anchor holds. It has always held. It will always hold.

We have this hope as an anchor for the soul, firm and secure.

Hebrews 6:19

Lord, You are my anchor. Firm and secure. When everything around me is shifting, You hold me fast. I trust the anchor today. It holds. It always holds. Amen.

CHAPTER 91

You Are Not Alone in This

From the Gardener

Dear one, the enemy's greatest weapon is isolation. He wants you to believe that you are the only one fighting this battle, the only one carrying this weight, the only one who hurts this badly. But you are not alone. You have never been alone.

The Lord is close to the brokenhearted and saves those who are crushed in spirit. Close, beloved. Not distant. Not watching from far away with folded arms. Close. Right next to you. Closer than the tears on your cheeks. Closer than the breath in your lungs.

And beyond My presence, I have placed others on this journey with you. Fellow branches in the tree. People who know what it is to be grafted in, who know what the cut feels like, who know what it means to draw from the root. You are part of a family now, dear one. Lean on them. Let them lean on you.

The Lord is close to the brokenhearted and saves those who are crushed in spirit.

Psalm 34:18

Father, thank You for being close to me in my brokenness. Thank You for the family You have placed around me. Break the lie of isolation. I am not alone. You are here, and Your people are with me. Amen

CHAPTER 92

After the Rain

From the Gardener

The storm is passing, beloved. Can you feel it? The wind is dying down. The clouds are thinning. The first ray of light is breaking through, and it is more beautiful than any sunrise you have ever seen, because this one comes after the rain.

I set My rainbow in the clouds as a sign of My covenant between Me and you and all living creatures. The rainbow is not just a pretty thing in the sky, dear one. It is My promise, painted in light and water, declaring to the universe: I keep My word. I will not let the flood destroy you. You will survive. You will thrive. You will see beauty again.

After the rain, the air is cleaner. The colors are brighter. The earth smells like new life. And you, beloved—you are stronger, clearer, more alive than you were before the storm began.

I have set my rainbow in the clouds, and it will be the sign of the covenant between me and the earth.

Genesis 9:13

Lord, I see the rainbow. I receive Your promise. The storm did not destroy me—it revealed Your faithfulness. Thank You for beauty after the rain. Amen.

CHAPTER 93

Stand Firm, Dear One

From the Gardener

Beloved, put on the full armor of God so that you can take your stand against the enemy's schemes. This battle is real. The opposition is real. But so is your armor, and so is the God who forged it for you.

After you have done everything, stand. Not run. Not hide. Not crumble. Stand. With the belt of truth around your waist, the breastplate of righteousness in place, your feet fitted with the gospel of peace, the shield of faith in your hand, the helmet of salvation on your head, and the sword of the Spirit—My word—in your grip.

You are equipped, dear one. You are armed. You are dangerous to the enemy and precious to Me. Stand firm. Do not give an inch. The battle belongs to the Lord, and the Lord has already won.

Therefore put on the full armor of God, so that when the day of evil comes, you may be able to stand your ground, and after you have done everything, to stand.

Ephesians 6:13

Lord, I put on Your armor today. Truth. Righteousness. Peace. Faith. Salvation. Your Word. I stand firm in Your strength. The battle belongs to You. Amen.

CHAPTER 94

The Roots Held

From the Gardener

Look back, beloved. Look at the storms you have already survived. The ones that felt like they would kill you. The ones you were sure you would not make it through. You are still here. You are still standing. The roots held.

He lifted me out of the slimy pit, out of the mud and mire; He set my feet on a rock and gave me a firm place to stand. That is your testimony, dear one. You were in the pit, and He pulled you out. You were in the mud, and He set you on a rock. Your feet are firm. Your footing is sure. And it is because the roots held.

The next storm? The roots will hold through that one, too. And the one after that. And the one after that. Because the root that supports you is the same root that has held every branch through every storm since the beginning of time. And it has never, ever failed.

He lifted me out of the slimy pit, out of the mud and mire; he set my feet on a rock and gave me a firm place to stand.

Psalm 40:2

Father, the roots held. Through every storm, every pit, every season of mud and mire—the roots held. Thank You for the firm place to stand. I trust the roots will hold through whatever comes next. Amen.

CHAPTER 95

Every Storm Made You Stronger

From the Gardener

Beloved, the storms you hated are the storms that built you. Every gust of wind that tried to break you actually strengthened your fibers. Every rain that tried to drown you actually deepened your roots. Every season of cold that tried to kill you actually prepared you for a spring you could not have survived without the winter.

Blessed is the one who perseveres under trial because, having stood the test, that person will receive the crown of life that the Lord has promised to those who love Him. The crown is not given to those who avoided the trial, dear one. It is given to those who persevered through it.

You are a perseverer. You are a survivor. You are a storm-tested, wind-proven, rain-soaked, still-standing child of the Most High God. And every storm made you stronger.

Blessed is the one who perseveres under trial because, having stood the test, that person will receive the crown of life that the Lord has promised to those who love him.

James 1:12

Lord, thank You for the strength that came from the storms. I am stronger because of what I have been through. I persevere because You persevere with me. I look forward to the crown. Amen.

CHAPTER 96

Safe in the Cleft of the Rock

From the Gardener

Come here, beloved. Let Me hide you. There is a cleft in the rock—a secret place carved by My own hands—where I tuck you in when the world is too much. Where My glory passes by and My goodness covers you. Where nothing can reach you because I am the rock, and you are hidden inside Me.

When I passed by, I put you in the cleft of the rock and covered you with My hand. That is what I do for those I love, dear one. I shelter you in the solid places. I cover you with My own body. I stand between you and the storm and say, "You cannot have this one."

Rest in the cleft, beloved. You are hidden. You are covered. You are safe. The storm rages outside, but in here, there is only My presence, My warmth, My love.

When my glory passes by, I will put you in a cleft in the rock and cover you with my hand until I have passed by.

Exodus 33:22

Father, hide me in the cleft of the rock. Cover me with Your hand. I rest in the secret place of Your presence. I am safe here. I am loved here. Thank You. Amen.

PART NINE

The Eternal Garden

The eternal promise. Heaven. The garden restored. The tree of life. Forever grafted into God's heart. The story does not end—it blooms into eternity.

CHAPTER 97

The Garden Restored

From the Gardener

Beloved, the story that began in a garden will end in a garden. Eden was not a mistake. It was a blueprint. A promise of what I always intended for you—unbroken fellowship, unhindered beauty, unending life. And what was lost in the first garden will be restored in the last.

The angel showed me the river of the water of life, as clear as crystal, flowing from the throne of God and of the Lamb down the middle of the great street of the city. On each side of the river stood the tree of life, bearing twelve crops of fruit, yielding its fruit every month. The tree of life, beloved. Not the tree of the knowledge of good and evil—the tree of *life*. And you are grafted into it.

The garden is waiting, dear one. And it is more beautiful than anything you could imagine. Every flower that ever wilted will bloom there forever. Every fruit that was ever stolen will hang heavy on the branches. And you will walk there with Me, as we were always meant to walk—together, in the cool of the day, forever.

Then the angel showed me the river of the water of life, as clear as crystal, flowing from the throne of God and of the Lamb down the middle of the great street of the city. On each side of the river stood the tree of life, bearing twelve crops of fruit, yielding its fruit every month.

Revelation 22:1–2

Lord, I long for the garden restored. Thank You for the promise of eternity with You—unbroken, unhindered, unending. Until then, I walk with You here, knowing that the best is yet to come. Amen

CHAPTER 98

No More Thorns

From the Gardener

A day is coming, beloved, when every thorn will be removed. Every thorn that ever pierced your skin, every brier that ever tangled your feet, every weed that ever choked your joy—all of it will be gone. Because I wore the crown of thorns so that you could walk free of them forever.

He will wipe every tear from your eyes. There will be no more death or mourning or crying or pain, for the old order of things has passed away. No more. Not reduced. Not managed. Eliminated. Gone. Finished. The curse is reversed, the thorns are burned, and all that remains is beauty and life and joy without end.

Hold on, dear one. The thorns are temporary. The garden is eternal. And the day is coming when the only thing you will feel under your feet is soft, green, deathless grass stretching out forever in every direction.

He will wipe every tear from their eyes. There will be no more death or mourning or crying or pain, for the old order of things has passed away.

Revelation 21:4

Jesus, thank You for wearing the crown of thorns so I could be free. I long for the day when every tear is wiped away and every thorn is removed. Until then, I hold onto Your promise. Amen.

CHAPTER 99

I Prepared a Place

From the Gardener

Beloved, where I am going, I am preparing a place for you. A real place. Not a metaphor. Not a concept. A room in My Father's house with your name on it, designed by the same hands that shaped the galaxies, decorated with the colors that make your heart sing.

I would not have told you if it were not true. I do not make empty promises. When I say I am preparing a place, I mean that right now, at this very moment, heaven is under construction—and your room is being built with eternal materials and infinite love.

And when it is ready, I will come back for you Myself. Not send an angel. Not leave directions. I will come. Personally. And I will take you home, so that where I am, you may be also.

Your room is almost ready, dear one. And it is beautiful.

My Father's house has many rooms; if that were not so, would I have told you that I am going there to prepare a place for you?
John 14:2

Jesus, thank You for preparing a place for me. Thank You that You will come back for me Yourself. I long for the day I see it. Until then, I trust Your promise. Amen.

CHAPTER 100

Eternal Roots

From the Gardener

The roots that sustain you are eternal, beloved. They do not age. They do not weaken. They do not decay. They reach into the very heart of God, and God has no end. Your connection to Me is not a temporary arrangement. It is an everlasting covenant, sealed in blood, ratified by resurrection, guaranteed by the Holy Spirit.

For God so loved the world that He gave His one and only Son, that whoever believes in Him shall not perish but have eternal life. Eternal. Not long. Not extended. Eternal. Life without end. Life beyond death. Life that stretches into forever and never, ever stops.

You are grafted into something that will outlast the stars, dear one. When the sun burns out and the mountains crumble and the oceans evaporate, you will still be alive, still connected, still drawing from the root that has no end.

For God so loved the world that he gave his one and only Son, that whoever believes in him shall not perish but have eternal life.

John 3:16

Father, my roots are eternal. My connection to You will never end. Thank You for eternal life—not just in length, but in depth. I am grafted into forever. Amen.

CHAPTER 101

The River of Life

From the Gardener

There is a river, beloved, whose streams make glad the city of God. A river of crystal, flowing from My throne, carrying the water of life to every corner of the eternal garden. And on the banks of this river, the trees of life grow—the trees into which you have been grafted.

This river never runs dry. It never slows. It never muddles or pollutes. It flows clear and pure and sweet from the heart of God, and it will flow forever. And you will drink from it, dear one. You will stand at its banks and cup the water in your hands and drink until your soul is satisfied in a way it has never been before.

The river is coming, beloved. And once you taste its water, you will forget every thirst you ever knew.

Then the angel showed me the river of the water of life, as clear as crystal, flowing from the throne of God and of the Lamb.

Revelation 22:1

Lord, I thirst for the river of life. Let me drink deeply of Your presence even now, and give me the hope of drinking from the crystal river that flows from Your throne forever. Amen.

CHAPTER 102

Every Branch Will Sing

From the Gardener

There is a day coming, beloved, when every branch in the tree will sing. Not just whisper. Not just sway. Sing. A song of joy so deep and full that the mountains will echo it and the heavens will tremble with the beauty of it.

Let the fields be jubilant, and everything in them; let all the trees of the forest sing for joy. The trees will sing, dear one. And you are one of those trees. You—the wild branch that was grafted in, the one who thought you did not belong—you will lift your voice with all the others and you will sing.

And the song will be about grace. About the Gardener who walked the hillside. About the cut that saved you. About the sap that healed you. About the love that never let you go. And the song will never, ever end.

Let the fields be jubilant, and everything in them; let all the trees of the forest sing for joy.

Psalm 96:12

Lord, I want to sing. Even now, even here, I lift my voice to You. And one day, in the eternal garden, I will sing the song that never ends. Thank You for giving me a reason to sing. Amen.

CHAPTER 103

You Will See My Face

From the Gardener

Beloved, right now you see Me dimly, as if looking through frosted glass. You sense My presence. You hear My voice. You feel My hand. But you have not yet seen My face. And oh, dear one, when you do—when you finally, fully, face-to-face see Me—everything will make sense.

For now we see only a reflection as in a mirror; then we shall see face to face. Now I know in part; then I shall know fully, even as I am fully known. The questions that haunt you now will dissolve. The pain that confuses you will suddenly make sense. Every "why" will be answered by My face.

I cannot wait for that day, dear one. The day you see Me as I truly am, and you realize that the God who grafted you in is more beautiful than anything your earthly eyes could have imagined.

For now we see only a reflection as in a mirror; then we shall see face to face. Now I know in part; then I shall know fully, even as I am fully known.

1 Corinthians 13:12

Jesus, I long to see Your face. Until then, I trust what I cannot yet see. And when the glass is finally clear, I know that every question will be answered by the beauty of who You are. Amen.

CHAPTER 104

The Scar Becomes a Crown

From the Gardener

Every scar you carry, beloved, will one day become a jewel in your crown. The places where you were cut, the wounds that ached for years, the marks that you tried to hide from the world—they will be transformed into something so radiant that the angels will weep at the beauty of it.

I consider that our present sufferings are not worth comparing with the glory that will be revealed in us. Not worth comparing. The pain you feel right now, as real as it is, will one day be eclipsed so completely by the glory that follows that it will seem like a shadow compared to the sun.

Your scars are being redeemed, dear one. They are being woven into a crown that will never tarnish, never fade, never lose its luster. And when you lay it at My feet—because I know you will, beloved—it will be the most beautiful thing in all of heaven. Because it was forged in suffering and polished by grace.

I consider that our present sufferings are not worth comparing with the glory that will be revealed in us.

Romans 8:18

Lord, transform my scars into crowns. Let my suffering produce a glory that I will lay at Your feet with joy. The pain is real, but the glory that is coming is greater. I believe it. Amen.

CHAPTER 105

Grafted for Eternity

From the Gardener

This graft, beloved, is not temporary. It is not a seasonal arrangement. It is not a trial period that might be revoked if you fail too many times. You are grafted into Me for eternity—permanent, irrevocable, sealed by the blood of the covenant.

Father, I want those You have given Me to be with Me where I am, and to see My glory. That is My prayer for you, dear one—the prayer I prayed before I went to the cross, the prayer that carries the weight of My own desire. I want you with Me. Not just for now. Not just for a lifetime. For ever and ever and ever.

Nothing will separate you from Me. Not in this life and not in the next. You are grafted into My heart, and My heart beats forever.

Father, I want those you have given me to be with me where I am, and to see my glory, the glory you have given me because you loved me before the creation of the world.

John 17:24

Jesus, I am grafted into You for eternity. Not for a season—forever. Your prayer is my hope: to be with You where You are, seeing Your glory. I hold onto that promise with everything I am. Amen.

CHAPTER 106

The Tree Will Never Fall

From the Gardener

Beloved, the tree you are grafted into will never fall. Kingdoms rise and kingdoms crumble. Empires blaze and empires fade. But the kingdom of God stands forever. The tree of life cannot be cut down, burned, toppled, or uprooted. It is eternal, because I am eternal.

In the time of those kings, the God of heaven will set up a kingdom that will never be destroyed, nor will it be left to another people. It will crush all those kingdoms and bring them to an end, but it will itself endure forever. This is the kingdom you belong to now, dear one. The unshakeable, unbreakable, everlasting kingdom.

When the world shakes, remember: the tree will never fall. When the nations tremble, remember: the tree will never fall. When everything that can be shaken is being shaken, you are grafted into the one thing that cannot be moved.

In the time of those kings, the God of heaven will set up a kingdom that will never be destroyed, nor will it be left to another people. It will crush all those kingdoms and bring them to an end, but it will itself endure forever.

Daniel 2:44

Father, Your kingdom will never be destroyed. Your tree will never fall. I am grafted into something eternal, and I rest in that unshakeable truth today. Amen.

CHAPTER 107

My Love Will Never End

From the Gardener

Beloved, I have loved you with an everlasting love. Not a love that expires. Not a love that fades with time. Not a love that grows tired or bored or disillusioned. Everlasting. As in: no end. As in: forever. As in: I will still be loving you when the stars have burned to nothing and the universe has folded in on itself and time has ceased to exist.

I have drawn you with unfailing kindness. Not because you earned it, but because My nature is love, and love is what I do. I cannot stop loving you any more than I can stop being God. It is who I am. It is what I am. And it is yours—unconditionally, irrevocably, eternally yours.

Rest in this, dear one. Whatever else changes, whatever else fails, whatever else disappoints—My love will never end. Never. I promise you with everything I am: My love will never, ever end.

The Lord appeared to us in the past, saying: 'I have loved you with an everlasting love; I have drawn you with unfailing kindness.'

Jeremiah 31:3

Lord, Your love has no end. I rest in that truth today. When everything else fails, Your love holds. When everything else changes, Your love remains. I am loved with an everlasting love. That is enough. Amen.

CHAPTER 108

Home at Last

From the Gardener

And now, beloved, we come to the end of the journey—and the beginning of forever. You have been wild, and you have been grafted. You have been cut, and you have been healed. You have been broken, and you have been made whole. You have weathered storms and borne fruit and grown taller than you ever imagined possible.

And one day—one beautiful, breathtaking, tear-erasing day—you will hear a voice from the throne saying, *"Look! God's dwelling place is now among the people, and he will dwell with them. They will be his people, and God himself will be with them and be their God."*

Home at last, dear one. Home at last. No more wandering. No more wondering. No more aching for a place to belong. You are home, and you will never leave again. The wild branch has found its forever tree. The Gardener has brought His work to completion. And it is very, very good.

Welcome home, beloved. Welcome home forever.

And I heard a loud voice from the throne saying, 'Look! God's dwelling place is now among the people, and he will dwell with them. They will be his people, and God himself will be with them and be their God. He will wipe every tear from their eyes. There will be no more death or mourning or crying or pain, for the old order of things has passed away.'

Revelation 21:3–4

Jesus, I am home. Home in You—now and forever. Thank You for grafting me into Your heart. Thank You for never letting me go. Thank You that the

story does not end—it blooms into eternity. I love You. I am Yours. Forever. Amen.

AFTERWORD

Dear Beautiful Friend,

If you've made it to this page, I want you to know something: you've come a long way. Whether you read these words in one sitting or slowly, one chapter at a time, you chose to show up. You opened your heart to the voice of the One who loves you most — and that takes courage.

When the storms return — and they will, because this world is both beautiful and broken — come back to these pages. Turn to the chapter your heart needs that day. Let the words wash over you again, fresh and alive, because truth never fades.

And if you know someone who needs to hear these words — someone growing wild on a rocky hillside, someone who feels cut off or forgotten — would you share this book with them? Sometimes the greatest gift we can give is the reminder that they are seen. That they are loved. That the Gardener has been watching them all along, with gentle hands and a plan that will take their breath away.

You are grafted in, beloved. You always will be. The root supports you. The sap sustains you. The tree will never fall. And the Gardener's hands will never let you go.

With gentle love,

Dana

You are grafted in, beloved.

You always will be.

www.ingramcontent.com/pod-product-compliance
Ingram Content Group UK Ltd.
Pitfield, Milton Keynes, MK11 3LW, UK
UKHW041639190726
13854UKWH00006B/2597

9 780999 177969